STUDIES IN THE PERSONAL SOCIAL SERVICES: NO 1

Series Editors: OLIVE STEVENSON and MICHAEL HILL

SOCIAL WORK AND MONEY

Studies in the Personal Social Services

2   CHILD ABUSE : ASPECTS OF INTERPROFESSIONAL
CO-OPERATION
by Christine Hallett and Olive Stevenson

Social Work and Money

MICHAEL HILL
and
PETER LAING

London
GEORGE ALLEN & UNWIN
Boston   Sydney

First published in 1979

GEORGE ALLEN & UNWIN LTD
40 Museum Street, London WC1A 1LU

© George Allen & Unwin (Publishers) Ltd, 1979

British Library Cataloguing in Publication Data

Hill, Michael James, b.1937
    Social work and money. - (Studies in the
    personal social services; no.1).
    1. Public welfare - Great Britain
    2. Economic assistance, Domestic - Great
    Britain
    I. Title II. Laing, Peter   III. Series
    362.5'0941   HV245   79-40683

    ISBN 0-04-360051-4
    ISBN 0-04-360052-2 Pbk

Typeset in 10 on 11 point Times by Brian Robinson, North Marston, Bucks.
and printed in Great Britain
by Unwin Brothers Ltd, Old Woking, Surrey

Preface

This book, together with *Child Abuse: Aspects of Interprofessional Co-operation* by Christine Hallett and Olive Stevenson, is the first of a series of short books which explicate key areas of concern for the organisation and practice of social work in local authorities. The books are designed for practitioners and for social work students.

The idea for a series of this kind came about from our concern to secure wider discussion of issues which arose during a study of field work in social services departments. This project, funded by the Department of Health and Social Security, the Scottish Social Work Services Group and the Northern Ireland Department of Health and Social Services was directed by Olive Stevenson and Phyllida Parsloe. Its main findings were published by HMSO in *Social Services Teams: The Practitioner's View*. None of the books in this series directly duplicate that report, but some of the issues in them were first discussed there and some of the data quoted in them emerged from that research and may have been reported there.

The authors of this book would like to thank DHSS and HMSO for permission to quote from the findings of the research. Special thanks are also due to Olive Stevenson as the director of the projects on which the book is based, and for her key role in stimulating thinking on these issues particularly through her earlier *Claimant or Client?* The authors are also grateful to all their colleagues in the research team for their help and advice, and also to many others who helped them in their work. From the latter group they would like to single out for mention Tony Emmett, Jim Spencer, Michael Valencia and Michael Jackson, together with the many social workers who co-operated with the field studies. Finally thanks are due to Michael Holdsworth of Allen and Unwin for his encouragement with this book, and indeed with the idea for the whole series.

Michael Hill
Peter Laing

Contents

Chapter 1

The Place of Help with Material Problems within Social Work

INTRODUCTION

This book is concerned with the impact of clients' financial and material problems upon social work practice in local authorities. Many people come to social services departments for assistance with financial difficulties, or for help with other problems which are nevertheless compounded by poverty and debts. Social workers have a range of options open to them for dealing with clients' financial problems. They may secure payments in cash from their department's own funds. They may be able to provide assistance in kind, telephones for the housebound elderly, or aids and house adaptations for the disabled, for example. They may be able to draw upon charitable sources of help, for example, hospital amenity funds or direct donations from voluntary societies. They may have stores of clothes, food and household goods that they have collected from voluntary sources. But above all they may intervene on the client's behalf, either with another agency who can help, or with organisations to whom he is in debt. The main helping agency they are likely to approach is the Supplementary Benefits Commission. The main creditor agencies with whom they have to intervene are the fuel boards and the housing authorities. These interventions may simply involve advising the client to press his own case further, but they are more likely to entail telephoning or writing to pursue the matter for him. Where appeal systems operate they may include advocacy at tribunals.

It is important to be quite clear at the outset that social workers are faced by people with a wide variety of material problems to which they make a range of responses. Thus arguments about whether social workers should or should not give out money need to be related to the various strategies they may adopt to help clients solve material problems, to aid and advocacy on the one hand and to help with budgeting on the other.

Over and above these issues, questions must be raised both about the nature of the social work task and about the functions of social services departments. The first and last chapters of this book will deal particularly with these wider questions of the contexts of the specific issues which are the concern of the middle chapters. The first will take the form of a relatively detached, scene-setting exercise. The last will take up rather more forcefully the underlying arguments about the implications of the problems discussed for the social work task within local government.

This book draws heavily upon, but is not limited by, the findings of two related research projects. One of these was a large, wide-ranging study of the social work task, as perceived by team members in a cross-section of areas from local authorities in all parts of the United Kingdom. Related volumes in the same series as this book deal with the many other issues raised by this research. The other project was concerned with money payments made by local authorities in England under Section 1 of the Children and Young Persons Act, 1963. This study sought to explore the reasons for individual payments and the significance for decisions of this kind of the boundary between social services and the Supplementary Benefits Commission.

MATERIAL PROBLEMS AND THE SOCIAL WORK TASK

Butrym (1976), drawing heavily on an unpublished paper by Butler, portrays clients of social services departments as having needs falling into four categories. Only one of the categories of need is seen as falling clearly within the social work remit: need for 'provision for the quality of inner life'. A second category, need 'for support and containment', is seen as partly a social work problem, partly a need for community or voluntary support. The other two categories of need are the primary concern of this book. On these Butrym and Butler take a firm stand, referring to a 'fundamental failure on the part of many people to differentiate social work from other social services'. It is appropriate to quote Butrym (pp.10-11) at some length on these (the internal quotations are from Butler's paper). The two categories of need referred to are:

(i)   *Those 'beyond the agency's remit',* for example 'housing, poverty, unemployment and other major areas of social difficulty'. Social services departments 'were not set up to deal with such difficulties and have neither the sanction nor resources to try to do so'. The social worker's task in relation to these needs is to transmit them to appropriate institutions and to press for the necessary changes in policies and provisions on the basis of real information available to them.

(ii) *'Matters of Right or Entitlement'*. These, according to Butler, refer to 'the major service-giving elements of social services departments: meals on wheels, clubs, transport, bath rails, home helps, information and advice, the whole range of aids and aides, to enable people to live more comfortably and with less stress'. Whilst social workers need to know 'the range of services available, who to contact, and how, where to find the necessary information', the actual administration of these various services is not part of the social workers' task.

Butrym's book has been described as 'a lament for times past rather than a blueprint for the future' (Burton, 1977). It is a reassertion of a view of the social work task which was very much more widespread in the forties and fifties than it is today. Yet it is a view that is given renewed force by the fact that social workers undoubtedly need to find ways of distinguishing between more and less appropriate tasks amongst the multiplicity of roles they are expected to perform today.

Burton's verdict on Butrym is clearly influenced by the extent to which social workers have sought to give increasing attention to practical and material problems, perhaps at the same time playing down their traditional concern with the 'quality of inner life'. One book which particularly influenced this shift in perspective was Barbara Wootton's *Social Services and Social Pathology* (1959). This pointed out the weaknesses of much of the research and theory on deviancy and delinquency upon which approaches to social casework had been based. Towards the end of the book Wootton turned to criticise 'contemporary attitudes in social work'. She argued (p. 296):

The range of needs for which public or voluntary services now provide, and the complexity of relevant rules and regulations have become so great, that the social worker who has mastered these intricacies and is prepared to place this knowledge at the disposal of the public, and when necessary to initiate appropriate action, has no need to pose as a miniature psychoanalyst or psychiatrist: her professional standing is secured by the value of her own contribution.

Wootton's book was clearly of importance in drawing attention to the weaknesses of much of the social science 'knowledge' upon which some social work practice was founded. She also raised some important moral questions about the right to interfere in people's lives, and in particular about the right to do that when the problem which brought them to social work agencies was insufficient income or difficulty in obtaining access to some public service. But to do this she necessarily gave little attention to those other problems—child neglect, bereavement, mental illness, and so on —for which the 'common-sense' approach she advocated might not be adequate. She rightly warned social workers about posing as 'miniature psychiatrists' but here, interestingly, the earlier analysis in her book suggested that she might have little faith in real psychiatrists. Hence there are areas of concern to which medical practitioners give little attention, and may indeed have little to offer, where social workers are sometimes offering valuable help. Whether or not such help is founded upon scientific knowledge may be beside the point.

The thrust of much thinking about social work since Wootton's *Social Science and Social Pathology* has therefore been neither to reject her message nor to accept it in its entirety, but to seek ways to ensure that a concern with material problems, and with the giving of aid and advice, is integrated with other aspects of social work practice. This is the sense in which it was possible for the reviewer of Butrym's book to portray it as rather dated. This commitment to combining the different approaches reaches its most elaborated form in the literature on 'integrated social work methods'. Thus Pincus and Minahan (1977) offer a definition of social work which clearly rejects Butler and Butrym's attempt to narrow the range of social works tasks (p.78):

Social work is concerned with the interaction between people and their social environment which affects the ability of people to accomplish their life tasks, alleviate distress and realise their aspirations and values. The purpose of social work therefore is to (1) enhance the problem-solving and coping capacities of people, (2) link people with systems that provide them with resources, services and opportunities, (3) promote the effective and human operation of these sytems and (4) contribute to the development and improvement of social policy.

This approach to social work, then, rejects the compartmentalisation of the various problems faced by social work clients, with the personal and immediately interpersonal relationship issues separated from their wider social contexts. Yet in doing so it is clearly open to the alternative criticism that it makes the social work task too general, too open to those who expect social workers to respond to every kind of problem clients may bring to social services departments.

Jordan criticises the 'unitary' approach for colluding with the tendency for responsibilities to be loaded upon social workers without regard to any rationale, except that it is convenient for other people to delegate a ragbag of 'social' tasks to them. Jordan argues (1977, p. 448):

> Ever since the creation of local authority, social services departments, social workers have been in search of an overall rationale for the many disparate tasks they perform. Since 1970, they have taken over an enormous range of jobs previously done by policemen, probation officers, rent collectors, debt collectors, public assistance men, sanitary inspectors and the electricity boards, quite apart from all the very different tasks which were lumped together in the amalgamation of the children's, welfare and mental health departments. Other agencies sometimes have even wider notions of their powers. One batch of recent referrals by a city housing official included: 'Mrs X (aged 75) has just been moved into a corporation flat at the above address. We think she may need social work assistance, as she is only four feet tall.' Examples of problems that have been officially brought to social workers' attention elsewhere are: dogs hunting in packs, flags hung incorrectly on flagpoles, chip papers in a garden, and ill-fitting slippers.
>
> The most widely adopted resolution of this problem, both in theory and practice, has been an attempt to construct a grandiose unified structure which encompasses all these tasks. On the theoretical side, the unitary or integrated approach to social work has quickly become fashionable in planning, in training management and in social work education.

This discussion has identified three comparatively distinctive statements about the social work task: from Butrym and Butler, from Wootton, and from Pincus and Minahan. It has also suggested the kinds of criticism that are advanced against each of them. It is not the task of this book to choose between them, although it will suggest some of the issues and arguments that need to be considered in relation to the various approaches that may be adopted by local authority social workers. However, it would be quite wrong to suggest that the concept of the social work task should be influenced solely by the nature of the material problems which clients may bring to social workers. This book is only concerned with one part of the contemporary social work task. Writers like Barbara Wootton, and more recently Adrian Sinfield, were right to draw attention to the extent to which social workers are confronted by problems of poverty, and problems resulting from the ineffective functioning of other agencies designed to solve material problems. It does not necessarily follow that the solution of those problems should be the central concern of social workers. The answer to that lies in the extent to which there are other workers available to tackle these issues, and in the importance of other problems requiring social workers' attention. Some attention will be given here to the first of these points; the second is beyond this book's brief. Hence, while in the last chapter some suggestions will be made about patterns of organisation which may facilitate the giving of adequate attention to material problems, the whole case for the adoption of those measures must also depend upon their impact upon other aspects of social work practice.

THE HISTORICAL BACKGROUND

Any contemporary policy problem is set in a complex historical context. This book will not delve into that context in any detail, but it is important not to forget the emotive and symbolic importance of the legacy of public assistance and of Victorian charity for social workers who today confront clients with material problems, and to acknowledge the character of the alternative social policy system which has been developed in its place.

Jordan, in his book *Poor Parents,* emphasises the importance of the legislation in 1948, which abolished the Poor Law and created the children's departments, in the following way. Under the Poor Law the provision of material aid to the poor and the provision of wider welfare services, including social work, were combined within a single agency. Even the voluntary organisations which were concerned to offer supporting services to individuals and families with problems tended to develop social work skills against a background of a concern to prevent the abuse of charitable funds. Hence the abolition of the Poor Law liberated social work from the preoccupations of poor relief. The relief function of the Poor Law passed to the National Assistance Board. Local authorities were to set up welfare departments to take over institutional care, and the vague but generally dormant obligation to take other measures to promote the welfare of groups in the community such as the elderly or handicapped. At the same time the Curtis Committee, in recommending the creation of separate children's departments, argued: 'we find a strong impression that the stigma attached to public assistance ... is so clearly ingrained that only a completely new approach will enable the authorities to keep clear of it'.

Hence, for Jordan, the legislation of 1948 marks a 'high point'; the scene was set for the development of social services, and particularly social work, freed from the shackles of the Poor Law. While this was largely true of the services for children, the local authority welfare departments took over a range of institutions and services from the public assistance committees, and developed social work activities in close association with the provision of material benefits. The National Assistance Act gave them the responsibility to provide a variety of forms of assistance in kind. The local authorities were 'required to provide residential care for all persons who, by reason of age, infirmity or any other circumstance, are in need of care not otherwise available to them'. They could charge for this accommodation where people had sufficient means; hence in effect they had to impose a 'means test'. The Act also gave the local authorities power 'to make arrangements for promoting the welfare' of 'persons who are blind, deaf or dumb, and other persons who are substantially and permanently handicapped by illness, injury or congenital deformity or such other disabilities as may be prescribed by the Minister'.

These welfare departments were united with the children's departments by the Local Authority Social Services Act, 1970. However, in the years before reorganisation their powers to provide domiciliary and residential services were markedly developed. By 1971 they had built up a large corps of social workers, albeit largely untrained, to pass on to the new departments.

One important statute increasing this group of local authority responsibilities is the Chronically Sick and Disabled Persons Act, 1970. This Act requires local authorities to identify the disabled and to provide a variety of aids, adaptations and additional facilities such as telephones. The administration of these provisions requires social work staff, occupational therapists and others to assess needs, to operate means tests and sometimes to liaise with social security departments.

The new children's departments, set up in 1948, did not have comparable powers to give benefits in kind, except inasmuch as they were responsible for the provision of residential care for neglected or ill-treated children. However, they had to face some of the shortcomings of the new welfare state in another way, since many of the children for whom they were responsible came from seriously deprived families. These people were discovering that the brave new world created in the 1940s provided a less than complete service for the poor. The new profession of social workers began to recognise that they had to help solve problems of poverty before they could engage in any more sophisticated casework. Earlier in this chapter we quoted Barbara Wootton's argument, published in 1959, that this should be at the forefront of their concern. There is no clear evidence that it was ever not an important consideration for practising child care officers, whatever textbooks imported from America might suggest. They found that considerable amounts of time had to be spent helping clients to get adequate support from the National Assistance Board. Moreover, where their clients could not get such help, for example when the family breadwinner was in full-time work, they had to seek help from traditional voluntary sources.

Jean Packman effectively portrays the problem the departments faced as they became increasingly concerned to do 'preventative work' to keep children in their homes but lacked sources of material aid, as follows (1975, pp. 60-1):

> They experienced the frustration of recognising many family situations where cash or help in kind would greatly assist their preventative and rehabilitative efforts, yet there were no funds available for them to use. Some one-parent families would manage more comfortably if money could be given to them to make good day-care arrangements for their children while they worked. Re-establishing homeless families would get off to a better start if they moved to a house equipped with reasonable furniture and sufficient bedding, crockery and pots and pans. There was no sanction for such direct help to families under the Children's Act so departments had to exercise their ingenuity by indirect means. They could act as persuasive go-betweens to the National Assistance Board for families where the parent was not in work. For the poor wage-earning family there were charities and voluntary organisations with resources to be tapped. Dr Barnardo's, for instance, was developing a valuable 'auxiliary boarding-out scheme' which helped unsupported mothers

financially instead of taking children into care. Sometimes a charity could be persuaded to clear debts, to help a family make a fresh start. The WVS was a valuable source of second-hand clothing and household equipment. Alternatively departments ... built up their own stores, persuading church congregations, local traders and their own foster parents to hand on discarded cots and prams, clothing, toys and household goods and even food, at Christmas, to be given to families who were known to be needy. In this way they acted very much as the voluntary casework agencies had always done, having few resources beyond social work manpower, but using that manpower to beg, borrow or persuade material goods and money from others, on their clients' behalf.

Packman's description of the situation which developed in the children's department holds true today, giving a good idea of the range of ways in which social workers seek to meet material needs. But, as a result of the concern expressed at that time about the lack of powers to give money, the Children and Young Persons Act, 1963, contained, in Section 1, the following provisions:

It shall be the duty of every local authority to make available such advice, guidance and assistance as may promote the welfare of children by diminishing the need to receive children into or keep them in care ... or to bring children before a juvenile court; and any provisions made by a local authority under this subsection may, if the local authority thinks fit, include provisions for giving assistance in kind or, in exceptional circumstances, in cash.

In Scotland local authorities were similarly given powers to make money payments under the Social Work (Scotland) Act, 1968, but an interesting difference is that the powers were more loosely defined, without the reference solely to the prevention of the need to take children into care. Section 12 of that Act specifies: 'It shall be the duty of every local authority to promote social welfare by making available advice, guidance and assistance on such a scale as may be appropriate for their area ... and such assistance may be given ... in kind or cash ...' . In the Scottish legislation the limitations are (1) that the assistance should be justified either by the fact that it will prevent a child coming into care (or being referred to a children's hearing) or that it will prevent the authority incurring greater expense by giving assistance in some other form, and (2) 'that regard shall be given' to the availability of assistance from other sources.

Jordan portrays the introduction of money powers, under these statutes, as fundamentally undermining the separation of income maintenance from social work, achieved in 1948. He sees this as opening the door for a return to the principles of the Poor Law (1974, pp. 103-4):

> The public welfare agency which is being created on the American model ... invites people to apply to it by virtue of their poverty and then treats them as maladjusted. It is more controlling and intrusive than any bureaucratically administered system of benefits. Starting from an assumption about the moral inferiority of the poor, it proceeds logically to the conclusion that the benefits made available to them should be conditional upon supervision by authorities concerned with moral improvement. It mops up an untidy problem from the income maintenance services in a way which is consistent with the principles of 'less eligibility'.

Jordan sees the setting up of integrated social services departments as perceived by social workers as designed to give 'rise to a family casework service' but instead re-creating 'first in structure, and now increasingly in function, the Public Assistance Committee of the 1930s'. Yet to integrate the children's departments, with their strong orientations to 'professional' social work, with the welfare departments, with their heavy commitments to the provision of other forms of aid, at a time when both politicians and the public were pressing for more material benefits for groups like the elderly and disabled, was bound to create a tension between social work and social services. Factors outside the departments have increased that tension, in particular the growing complexity of the other social services and the pressure on all services to ration the benefits they have to offer. To single out the issue of money powers from the other material issues and problems with which social workers have to deal helps us to focus on one particularly difficult development in the evolution of local authority social work. It is an issue that will be given special attention in this book. But it is misleading to emphasise it alone as a source of social worker involvement with clients' money problems, when there are many others.

CONCLUSIONS

In the earlier part of this chapter a brief account was given of the way in which controversy over work on clients' material problems has occurred in discussions of the nature of the social work task. In the second half of the chapter a historical perspective was provided on the place occupied by this issue in the development of social work and of the role of the social services department. In both sections it was made clear that the issues with which this book is concerned are deeply entangled with problems and controversy about the role of the social worker.

The issues to be discussed here are political, in more than one sense. At the heart of the tension within social work, as it emerged from its nineteenth-century origins, was a political controversy about the extent to which the poor were responsible for their own condition. Perspectives on social work which saw the solutions to the problems of poverty as lying with the poor themselves—more effort to find work, better budgeting, and so on—clearly led to a different view of the social work role than perspectives which blamed social and economic conditions external to the poor. Perspectives which involved an emphasis upon psychological problems — personal maladjustment, problems with family dynamics and so on —have often been regarded as comparable to those perspectives which saw solutions to depend upon greater personal efforts by the poor. This is an oversimplification; such approaches might regard problems arising from the social structure as irrelevant, or they might disregard them. But they might equally regard them as problems needing sloution before 'real' casework could begin, or they might regard the sociological and psychological factors contributing to their clients' problems as inextricably intertwined. There has been, however, running through the debate about causation, ample scope for differences of opinion about the extent to which material problems should be tackled by social workers, and about the ways in which they should be tackled. Political differences are apparent both about the extent to which the public services should be concerned with the attack on poverty, and about the extent to which the social work profession should involve itself in that attack.

Yet the politics of the issues involved are seldom simple. Two examples may be taken, central to the discussion in this book, on which broadly similar activities by social workers may be invested with very different significance by both social workers and clients. First, a money payment under Section 1 of the Children and Young Persons Act, 1963, may be seen as a desperate attempt to stem severe poverty in a situation in which no other agency will help. But it may equally be seen as a means, in a relationship between a social worker and a client, of giving a reward for approved behaviour. In such a situation it may play a part in the conditioning of an individual very similar to many of the charitable donations given by the Charity Organisation Society in the nineteenth century. Such a view of the function of Section 1 may be quite abhorrent to the social worker who sees his money-giving powers in the terms set out first above.

Secondly, many social workers intervene on their clients' behalf with local offices of the Supplementary Benefits Commission. Again such action may be conceived as part of a 'war against the system', designed to help the client get all he can from a reluctant state. Or it may be a paternalistic intervention to help someone who is deemed to be unable to help himself, but who needs a little encouragement if he is to be responsive to 'treatment'. These alternatives, and those discussed in the last paragraph, are rather extreme statements of some of the possibilities; there are many other motives for these actions which lie between the extremes. Social workers in local authorities cannot escape from a multitude of situations in which clients seek help with material problems. Yet they may make a wide variety of responses for a large number of reasons. The issues seem simple: whether or not to make a money payment, whether or not to intervene with another agency. But in fact they are often complex, and loaded with varied and difficult political significance.

Chapter 2

Money Payments by Social Services Departments

INTRODUCTION

In England and Wales most money payments provided by social services departments are made under the powers laid down in Section 1 of the Children and Young Persons Act, 1963. These were described in the last chapter. Reference was also made to Section 12 of the Social Work (Scotland) Act, 1968, which gives social workers rather wider powers to make payments to promote the welfare of clients, without the restrictions which limit payments of Section 1 to families where there is a danger of children becoming in need of reception into care. However, the main purposes for which Section 12 is used seem to be much the same as those for which Section 1 is used. The main distinctions in practice are more in the readiness with which cash is used than in the actual ways in which it is used. In Northern Ireland there are two relevant statutes. Section 164 of the Children and Young Persons Act (Northern Ireland), 1968, is modelled upon Section 1, while Article 15 of the Health and Personal Services (Northern Ireland) Order, 1972, is broadly comparable to Section 12. The social workers in Northern Ireland make comparatively little use of Article 15.

In some areas social workers also have access to limited amounts of money provided by charities or charitable gifts. In hospitals, in particular, there may be such funds available for grants to needy patients. Generally, however, the amount of money of this kind available is comparatively small. Social workers may, very exceptionally, make money payments to help young people recently released from local authority care. The scale of such transactions is so small as to be unimportant; therefore they will not be discussed further here.

This account of the issues arising in connection with the payment of money to clients will be primarily based upon the study of the use of Section 1 in England and Wales, together with information drawn from the interviews of social workers from throughout the United Kingdom in which, as part of the wider inquiry on the social work task, they were asked about their experience of, and attitudes to, money payments. An intensive study of the use of Section 12 in Scotland is being undertaken by Valencia and Jackson at Stirling University. While they have shared some of their findings with the authors, their final report is not, at the time of writing, available. There is little reason to expect that their findings will lead to a radically different interpretation of the way the issues with which this chapter is concerned are handled in Scotland.

While our own research findings are given primary attention in this chapter, both the way in which the research was designed and the way in which its results are interpreted were clearly influenced by earlier work on this topic. The main earlier discussions were Heywood and Allen's book *Financial Help in Social Work,* a study of Section 1 carried out in 1967, Handler's study of London children's departments reported in his *The Coercive Social Worker,* Jordan's polemical treatment of the money payments issue in his *Poor Parents* and Lister and Emmett's useful compilation of the available evidence on this topic in their CPAG pamphlet *Under the Safety Net.*

In the previous chapter some attention was given to the argument that the development of money-giving powers has tended to undermine the separation between the provision of material aid and the provision of social work support. Jordan and Handler have been the primary exponents of the view that this has introduced a new element of 'social control' into the relationships between social workers and their clients. Using evidence from Handler's study, and from the study by Heywood and Allen, Jordan argues (1974, pp. 103-4):

Handler's study of the work of three London children's departments in 1968 showed that the chief method employed for controlling clients' behaviour was the way in which a social worker dispensed rewards and benefits that families needed. The power to give cash under Section 1 of the 1963 Act was often used as a way of getting families to adopt standards which were considered to be more acceptable to the rest of the community, an exact parallel with Keith-Lucas's findings in American public welfare agencies. It was this power to give material assistance, rather than the threat of court proceedings, that was the first and most widely employed device in conflict regulation and social control. Bearing in mind the high proportion of referrals of children to social services departments that come from the parents themselves, and the fact that the Manchester research ...

suggests that more than half of all referrals require financial assistance or material aid, the power to give poor relief becomes quite evidently the most important weapon of authority in the social worker's armoury, and the shortage of resources for the purpose of relief becomes his most important motivation for exerting this control.

This issue of 'social control' has not been the only ground for disquiet about the powers given to social services departments under Section 1 and Section 12. Two other issues have been the extent to which, under these powers, social services departments are gradually taking over responsibilities to provide for 'exceptional needs' which would otherwise be met by the Supplementary Benefits Commission, and the extent to which local authorities use their discretion to make money payments in ways which vary markedly and inconsistently from authority to authority, area to area, and even from 'case' to 'case'. All the authors quoted above have drawn attention to these issues. Our own study largely substantiates the points they have made.

VARIATIONS IN THE USE MADE OF MONEY PAYMENTS

In the course of collecting child care statistics for England for the financial year 1974-5 the Department of Health and Social Security decided to ask for information on money payments under Section 1. This valuable experiment provides some useful insights into the variations in the use made of the powers. Inevitably, however, there were problems with this first attempt to secure detailed information on a subject on which some authorities kept very inadequate records. In 1974-5 all but eleven English social services departments (Cleveland, Newcastle, Lancashire, Cheshire, Wolverhampton, Islington, Lambeth, City of London, Cambridgeshire, East Sussex and West Sussex) provided some evidence on the use they made of Section 1. However, the returns varied in completeness and, it may be suspected, in accuracy; this should be taken into account in the following discussion. The national statistics only give a very general idea of the issues which are deserving of attention. To illustrate some of the variations in use of Section 1, examples of individual authorities have been quoted, but we would not wish these to be seen as forming the basis for 'league tables' encouraging invidious comparisons between authorities with very different policies. Indeed, as will be suggested later, there are significant perspectives on this issue which suggest that it may be as undesirable to be at the top as at the bottom of a league table of Section 1 payments.

There are very wide variations in the extent to which the authorities make use of their Section 1 powers. The authority making the highest use was Hackney, which made payments to 112.7 families per 10,000 population, paying out the equivalent of £1.79 for every person in the borough. The authority making the lowest use was County Durham which made payments to 1.2 families per 10,000 population, spending the equivalent of a tenth of a penny per head of population. Table 2.1 lists the authorities making the highest use of Section 1 and Table 2.2 lists those making the lowest use. Also included in the tables are figures for expenditure on social services as a whole per head and for numbers of fieldwork staff per 10,000 population. These also suggest wide variations between authorities and are included to inform the later discussion.

The statistics offer three possible indices of use of Section 1 powers: numbers of families given payments, numbers of payments made, and amounts of money paid out. One of the weaknesses of the statistics is that most authorities returned the same figures for numbers of families supported and numbers of payments made, yet a minority quoted figures for these two which diverged quite markedly. For example, Bury supported 162 families but made 231 payments. From our own investigation of local authority practice we would expect that nearly all authorities would quote quite different figures, yet few do. Hence, in this respect the figures are likely to be misleading.

The distinction between numbers of families supported and amounts of money paid out is an important one as Table 2.1 makes very clear. Hackney stands out as both a remarkably frequent payer and a remarkably high payer. Its average payment was £159.11. By contrast Rochdale and Sheffield, though willing to make many payments, made very small ones: averages £7.27 and £8.13 respectively.

The six authorities selected for the commissioned study of Section 1 were chosen to ensure the inclusion of authorities at various points along the continuum from the heaviest to the lightest users. However, although one authority (Northern Borough) made a comparatively large number of payments in this period, its payments were relatively small. No very high spender was included in the survey. Tables 2.3 and 2.4 illustrate this, and also demonstrate some of the variations between authorities in respect of the size of payments made.

Table 2.1 *Authorities making very high use of Section 1*

	Families supported per 10,000 population	Section 1 expenditure per head*	Total social services expenditure per head*	Fieldwork staff per 10,000 population
Hackney	112.7	£1.79	£32.92	6.3
Camden	93.6	£0.25	£43.74	13.1
Westminster	64.0	£0.15	£31.43	11.5
Tower Hamlets	59.5	£0.10	£41.21	12.1
Hammersmith	38.2	£0.69	£34.69	10.2
Southwark	33.4	£0.05	£35.00	10.4
Rochdale	30.6	£0.02	£12.81	4.4
Coventry	21.2	£0.05	£13.59	4.8
Lewisham	18.5	£0.04	£29.82	9.4
Kensington	18.4	£0.03	£27.24	9.6
Haringey	18.2	£0.10	£21.58	3.8
Sheffield	16.2	£0.01	£13.81	3.5
Newham	16.0	£0.03	£16.69	4.8
Avon	14.8	£0.09	£12.47	4.5
Oxfordshire	14.4	£0.13	£11.30	3.0

*i.e. amount spent divided by the authority's total population.

Table 2.2 *Authorities making very low use of Section 1*

	Families supported per 10,000 population	Total Section 1 expenditure	Total social services expenditure per head	Fieldwork staff per 10,000 population
Durham	1.2	£696	£10.42	2.7
Knowsley	1.4	£651	£12.86	3.8
Essex	1.6	£7,000	£8.73	2.9
Rotherham	1.7	£793	£9.43	3.5
Walsall	1.9	£2,111	n.k.	n.k.
Trafford	2.0	£864	£10.83	3.1
Surrey	2.0	£12,597	£8.73	2.7
Staffordshire	2.1	£5,858	£8.47	2.6
Solihull	2.1	£339	£6.71	3.7
Northumberland	2.3	£1,358	£10.12	3.4
St Helens	2.5	£403	£9.29	2.9

Note In this table, unlike Table 2.1, Section 1 expenditure has not been quoted per head of population as the very low amounts involved are, roughly speaking, merely fractions of one penny.

Table 2.3 *Variations in payment size between the survey authorities (payment size rounded to nearest pound, percentages in each size category included in brackets)*

	£0-4	£5-9	£10-14	£15-19	£20-49	£50+
Midlands Borough	39 (55)	15 (21)	6 (9)	4 (6)	6 (9)	1 (1)
Northern Borough 1	65 (64)	14 (14)	7 (7)	4 (4)	12 (12)	—
London Borough	9 (41)	2 (9)	2 (9)	2 (9)	4 (18)	3 (14)
Southern County	9 (26)	10 (29)	1 (3)	2 (6)	7 (20)	6 (17)
Northern County	60 (40)	27 (18)	12 (8)	8 (5)	31 (21)	13 (9)
Northern Borough 2	23 (45)	7 (14)	10 (20)	1 (2)	9 (18)	1 (2)

Table 2.4 reflects the variations in practice shown in Table 2.3 by relating payment numbers to payment size for each authority.

Table 2.4 *Payments made and amounts spent by the survey authorities*

	Number of payments	Amount spent	Average payment size	Families supported per 10,000 population
Midlands Borough	71	£566	£7.97	9.5
Northern Borough 1	102	£666	£6.53	19.4
London Borough	22	£381	£17.32	4.3
Southern County	35	£855	£24.43	1.4
Northern County	151	£2,510	£16.62	6.2
Northern Borough 2	51	£668	£13.10	5.9

These variations can be related to the variations in the purposes for which Section 1 payments were made. This will be discussed later. In Table 2.4 the figures for London Borough give a slightly misleading picture of the total use of Section 1 as almost half the money available went towards a special holiday fund for children. This fund was administered separately and we were not able to study individual allocations from it.

Table 2.5 provides evidence on a further variation in the use made of Section 1, that within individual authorities. In the table numbers of payments are set out for each social work area within the six authorities studied. In Northern County there were area allocations of money, weighted to take account of population. In

Southern County equal amounts were allocated to each area. In the other authorities, funds were allocated from a central pool and social workers were generally unaware of budgetary limits set for the authority as a whole. In the event of overspending it was presumed that headquarters might have to curb the use of Section 1 in the last months of the year, although no evidence was given to us of such a situation arising. Rather there was a tendency to underspend allocations. Table 2.4, therefore, reflects some considerable variations in practice from area to area. To some extent these variations may be explicable in terms of the populations served. It was hard to check this precisely. In the most striking example, that of Midlands Borough, where one area made more payments than the other four together, this issue was carefully examined. Workers within the authority thought that the five areas were comparatively well matched in terms of caseloads and in the intensity of social problems. In general it was a remarkably homogeneous borough.

Table 2.5 *Variations in numbers of payments between areas within the survey authorities (percentages in each area included in brackets)*

Area	Midlands Borough	Northern Borough 1	London Borough	Southern County	Northern County	Northern Borough 2
1	38 (54)	31 (30)	9 (41)	9 (26)	12 (18)	10 (20)
2	6 (9)	23 (23)	6 (27)	5 (14)	23 (15)	9 (18)
3	13 (18)	14 (14)	6 (27)	5 (14)	9 (6)	12 (24)
4	9 (13)	25 (25)	1 (5)	6 (17)	6 (4)	6 (12)
5	5 (7)	9 (9)		3 (9)	7 (5)	14 (28)
6				4 (11)	9 (6)	
7				2 (6)	2 (1)	
8				1 (3)	6 (4)	
9					6 (4)	
10					14 (9)	
11					19 (13)	
12					5 (3)	
13					9 (6)	
14					16 (11)	
15					8 (16)	

Some of the more striking variations were the result of particular areas making large numbers of small payments to meet immediate needs for money for food. Thus Area 1 in Midlands Borough made 63 per cent of all the payments for food in the borough but only 29 per cent of all the payments over £10. Similarly Area 5 in Northern Borough made 38 per cent of the payments for food but 19 per cent of the payments over £10.

Valencia and Jackson, in their study of Section 12 (n.d.), have suggested that, while socio-economic factors seem to have some influence upon variation in money payments in Scotland, other situational factors, which cannot be so readily quantified, are clearly of considerable importance. These are differences in policy both between authorities and within authorities. We attempted a similar but more limited multi-variate analysis of the factors which might influence Section 1. The exercise was not developed elaborately because it was found that in England the special characteristics of the London authorities, and particularly of the inner London ones, had a distorting impact upon the data as a whole. Broadly, the inner London authorities stand out as high users of Section 1, were high spenders on social services, had high proportions of children in care and a high ratio of social work staff per head of population. Outside London the high Section 1 users were not particularly distinguished by high ratings on the other indices, and an inspection of the authorities outside London which figure in the lists in Tables 2.1 and 2.2 does not suggest any obvious pattern.

The picture is further complicated by the extent to which, in 1974-5, some authorities were incurring heavy Section 1 expenditure on the prevention of homelessness. To some degree this explains the very high figures for central London. The DHSS statistics did not provide a category for the classification of this use of Section 1. 'Arrears of rent' was classified but board and lodging payments had to be included in the 'others' category in the statistics. Significantly, 71 per cent of Hackney's payments came in the 'others' category.

Outside London, however, there were some surprising variations between authorities which are unlikely to be explicable in terms of differential spending on the homeless. Why, for example, should Sheffield be in Table 2.1 as a very high user of Section 1 and Rotherham in Table 2.2 as a very low user? Why should Rochdale have supported 30.6 families per 10,000 population in this way but Oldham only 6.2 families? Or Oxfordshire have made 14.4 payments per 10,000 while Essex made 1.6? Any further exploration of the reasons for these variations must take more fully into account the purposes for which payments were made.

THE PURPOSES OF MONEY PAYMENTS

The interviews of social workers suggested that, in Scotland and Northern Ireland as much as in England and Wales, money was primarily used to rescue families facing emergencies. The purposes of payments fell into four main categories: help with problems arising from a lack of money to meet immediate needs for food and other household necessities, assistance with debts to fuel boards where the termination of supply was threatened, help with other debts, of which rent arrears were the most common example, and measures to prevent homelessness.

Table 2.6 provides information on the way the six English local authorities whose Section 1 policies and practices were studied in detail used their money.

Table 2.6 *Purposes for which each authority made Section 1 payments (percentage of the total number of payments made by the authorities included in brackets)*

Purpose of payment	Midlands Borough	Northern Borough 1	London Borough	Southern County	Northern County	Northern Borough 2
Food	35 (49)	67 (66)	10 (46)	14 (40)	51 (34)	16 (31)
Fuel	11 (16)	16 (16)	5 (23)	10 (29)	26 (17)	6 (12)
Holidays	2 (3)	1 (1)	0	0	5 (3)	0
Transport	5 (7)	3 (3)	1 (5)	2 (6)	9 (6)	6 (12)
Appliances	1 (1)	7 (7)	1 (5)	1 (3)	12 (8)	8 (16)
Clothing	3 (4)	0	0	1 (3)	11 (8)	3 (6)
Day care	4 (6)	1 (1)	4 (18)	4 (11)	13 (9)	5 (10)
Accommodation	3 (4)	4 (4)	1 (5)	2 (6)	11 (8)	5 (10)
Other	7 (10)	3 (3)	0	1 (3)	13 (9)	2 (4)

In Table 2.6 some of the users are expressed in shorthand form, so a little further explanation is needed. The category 'food' is what may be called, in supplementary benefits' terms, an 'urgent need payment'. That is to say, people had gone to social services departments claiming that they had no money to meet their ordinary living requirements. 'Holidays' includes subsidies to holidays for children or families. The 'transport' category is largely bus fares for various purposes. Included here are payments for bus fares to visit supplementary benefits offices! 'Appliances' are mainly grants for cookers; in this category are grants to secure calor gas stoves when other supplies of fuel had been cut off on account of unpaid bills. 'Day care' describes payments for the day care of children. 'Accommodation' includes help with rent arrears and payments for bed and breakfast.

Overall 45 per cent of all payments were for food, and 17 per cent were for fuel. However, it seemed to be the pressures upon them to make payments towards fuel bills which worried social services departments the most. Considerable efforts were being made to keep down the demands for help with fuel bills. This concern about fuel bills was perhaps partly a reflection of the fact that grants for this purpose were much larger than those for food. Seventy-six per cent of all food payments were under £5, whereas 89 per cent of all fuel payments were in excess of £10 and 15 per cent were even over £50. The other reason for particular anxiety about fuel bills was that this was clearly a growing problem, assuming more serious proportions at the time the authorities were being studied, in the first half of 1976, than when the payments studied were being made, in the second half of 1975. The fuel debt problem is discussed fully in the appendix.

While the fuel problem may be seen as an increasing source of concern, the evidence that such high percentages of Section 1 payments were to meet urgent needs for food brings up very starkly whether this was in conformity with the intention of the Act and whether a couple of pounds on a Friday evening, because some other payment had not come through, was really preventing the reception of children into care! Such payments, which, as will be shown below, were often made as loans, were surely merely preventing borrowing from a relative or neighbour. Family break-up or critical child neglect seems an unlikely consequence of failure to obtain a small sum of money from a public agency. These payments, too, bring into question very significantly the relationship between SBC payments and Section 1, which is explored in Chapter 3.

Since food and fuel payments take up such a high proportion of Section 1 budgets, more imaginative uses of this legislation are fairly rare. The practice of using money for holidays, which was particularly the case in the London Borough, seems to be a comparatively rare example of a more special use. Otherwise, the use of money for day care and a small expenditure in one authority (three payments of £5) for intermediate treatment were the only quantitatively significant cases where the requirements of the Act seemed to be operated in an imaginative way.

It must be acknowledged that the six English authorities studied did not include one where considerable Section 1 help had been given to the homeless. At the time of writing the transfer of responsibility for the homeless to the housing authorities in England, Wales and Scotland under the Housing (Homeless Persons) Act, 1977, is just taking place. It may be that this will relieve the considerable pressure upon social services agencies that was experienced wherever the housing departments had not followed the government's suggestions in its earlier Circular (Department of the Environment Circular 18/74). In Scotland this Circular had not been operative so a heavy social work department involvement in the provision of help to the homeless was general. In England and Wales there were, as already suggested, marked local variations. Many of the more rural counties had found the district councils particularly reluctant to provide for the homeless. Although overall the numbers of homeless families in such areas were seldom large, there were certain crucial pressure points. Perhaps the most salient of these were the seaside resort areas, which have accommodation readily available in winter and therefore attract the homeless from other areas, but experience in summer both an inflow of people seeking work and a scarcity of accommodation. The difficult time is the spring. At that time temporary tenants in holiday accommodation are evicted just as other families come into the area in hope of work and accommodation.

At the time of writing, the extent to which the housing departments will be fulfilling their obligations under the new legislation is far from clear. If they take a comparatively narrow view of their statutory obligations, rigorously adopt the provision in the Act which enables them to refuse to help people deemed to have made themselves homeless and are slow to deal with emergencies, the social services departments will still have demands on their Section 1 and Section 12 resources. In any case, even where requests for money are rare they may find an increasing need to take on other work related to this key material resource problem: helping those in rent arrears to budget, assisting the homeless to press their rights to accommodation, and so on.

Social Work and Money

THE USE OF LOANS

Section 1 payments are widely given as loans rather than grants. Unfortunately the DHSS statistics provide no evidence on the extent of that practice, or on the extent to which loans are recovered. All six of the English local authorities studied encouraged the use of loans. Loans were also frequently given in the Scottish and Northern Irish authorities where social workers were interviewed.

Table 2.7 *Number of loans made by each authority classified by the purpose of payment (percentages of total payments for that purpose included in brackets)*

Purpose of payment	Midlands Borough	Northern Borough 1	London Borough	Southern County	Northern County	Northern Borough 2
Food	14 (40)	36 (54)	5 (50)	10 (71)	20 (39)	1 (6)
Fuel	5 (46)	5 (31)	0	2 (20)	16 (62)	3 (50)
Transport	0	2 (67)	0	0	1 (11)	2 (33)
Appliances	1 (100)	2 (29)	0	0	2 (17)	0
Accommodation	2 (67)	0	0	0	2 (18)	1 (20)
All purposes	24 (34)	46 (45)	5 (23)	12 (34)	48 (32)	7 (14)
% of loans which were payments for food	58	78	100	83	42	14
% which were payments for fuel	21	11	0	17	38	21

The figures in Table 2.7 give some idea of the wide variations in practice in the use of loans. The authorities differed in their readiness to make payments as loans rather than grants, and they also differed in the purposes for which loans were given. Within authorities there were marked differences between areas in the extent to which loans were used. Area 1 in Midlands Borough, which was responsible for 54 per cent of the payments from its authority, provided 75 per cent of its loans. All but one of the loans from London Borough were made by Area 1. Only three of the eight areas in Southern County made any loans at all. The smaller payments were likely to be made as loans. Of the payments under £5, 40 per cent were loans. However, a not insubstantial number of larger payments were regarded as loans. Of the payments between £10 and £49, 27 per cent were loans, and even 21 per cent of payments over £50. Forty-six loans (32 per cent) were fully recovered and a further thirteen (9 per cent) were recovered in part.

A considerable amount of confusion about the use of loans was revealed when policy on this was discussed with social work management staff. In Southern County, several divisional directors saw loans as a part of social work treatment, mentioning the opportunity to foster financial responsibility and suggesting that a loan might operate as a bond between social worker and client. It was not considered fair to others to give a grant to a particular client merely because he would be unlikely to pay a loan back. Yet many loans were not recovered, and were not followed up too strenuously for fear of damaging a relationship and because the collection of debt was too costly of time. In another of the authorities many payments were made initially as loans, but were reclassified as grants if recovery proved difficult in order to prevent pressure upon social workers from finance staff who were concerned to achieve recoveries. In Table 2.7 these are not shown as loans.

In Northern County, where fuel payments were commonly made as loans, one area office used repayment of loans as a sort of savings account for clients. Money repaid would be counted towards the next fuel bill presented to social services.

In many of the areas some social workers expressed unease about the use of loans, suggesting that indebtedness made social work relationships more difficult and that some clients avoided social workers when loans were outstanding. Many social workers were reluctant to get into situations in which they had to give considerable time to debt collecting. In general, therefore, there was a lack of consensus about loans policy, and considerable scope for controversy within departments on this issue.

WHO DECIDES ON MONEY PAYMENTS?

It is comparatively rare for basic grade social workers to have any formal powers to authorise payments. In the six English authorities whose Section 1 policies were studied none had this power as a matter of course, although in one case (Midlands Borough) the rules were comparatively lax about the circumstances in which a social worker might stand in for someone more senior in his absence. In only two of the authorities included in the social work task research were basic grade workers given discretion to make payments. One of these was a Scottish authority where grants up to £5 might be made under Section 12 of the Social Work (Scotland) Act. Even in this authority one of the teams had imposed their own limitations upon this power. They had decided that decisions should be taken by a committee consisting of the area officer (or one of the seniors in his absence), a qualified social worker and three others drawn from whoever was available (who might be other social workers or even trainees, ancillaries, or students on placement). The social worker whose case was under consideration completed an application form and presented the case to the committee. In the other authority, a Northern Irish board, one of the districts allowed social workers to pay up to £2. In this district, however, the social workers said that they very often consulted their team leader before making a payment.

In many of the teams studied social workers acknowledged that their team leaders generally accepted their recommendations for payment. The position was often like that for other aspects of supervision, that is, team leaders were content to 'rubber-stamp' the decisions of experienced staff in whom they had confidence whilst scrutinising the decisions of others. However, in several of the authorities studied team leaders had little or no discretion themselves. In one English county only the area director could authorise payments and even he had to submit proposals for expenditure of over £30 to the director. In one English borough only the director had power to make payments, and he had to consult the committee chairman and another member about payments over £50. In this authority, in emergencies, teams based away from headquarters could pay out a small petty-cash float.

Tables 2.8 and 2.9 give data on who authorised payments in the six English authorities in the special Section 1 study. These tables broadly reflect what has been said about formal limitations, but also show that some informal waiving of the rules did actually influence who authorised.

Table 2.8 *Position of person authorising payment by each authority (percentage of total payments made by the authority included in brackets)*

Position of person authorising	Midlands Borough	Northern Borough 1	London Borough	Southern County	Northern County	Northern Borough 2
Social worker	5 (7)	1 (1)	0	0	2 (1)	0
Team leader	22 (31)	49 (48)	9 (41)	0	21 (14)	3 (6)
Area management	42 (59)	48 (47)	9 (41)	16 (46)	111 (74)	46 (90)
Director or headquarters	0	0	4 (19)	18 (52)	17 (11)	2 (4)
Chairman or committee	0	4 (4)	0	0	0	0
Unclear	2 (3)	0	0	1 (3)	0	0

Table 2.9 *Position of person authorising payment by amount of payments (percentage of total payment of that amount included in brackets)*

Position of person authorising	£0-4	£5-19	£20-49	£50+
Social worker	6 (3)	1 (1)	0	1 (4)
Team leader	73 (54)	28 (21)	3 (4)	0
Area management	123 (61)	96 (72)	48 (69)	5 (22)
Director or headquarters	1 (0)	8 (6)	15 (22)	17 (74)
Chairman or committee	0	1 (1)	3 (4)	0

It also seems comparatively rare for individual social work areas to have their own budgets for money payments. Most of the examples of this which we found came from the more decentralised authorities in Scotland and Northern Ireland. It has already been pointed out that only two of the six English authorities above had area allocations, the two counties.

It was quite clear from the interviews with basic grade social workers that within individual teams there may be great variations in the use of money. Clearly the methods by which the hierarchies control expenditure help to prevent even greater variations in payments. But this is essentially a negative control; it works to prevent payments in circumstances in which social workers think payment should be made, but not to force the making of grants when social workers have decided they are not appropriate. Social workers are confronted by many clients with money problems. In some cases those clients may know of the money-giving powers and may actually ask for help. If social workers say 'no' that is normally the end of the matter. In a few cases social workers may consult their team leaders on whether they are right to say 'no', but in no sense can they be said to be processing 'applications' for help from clients who must be given formal decisions. Moreover, in many cases consideration of the possibility of a money payment will be upon the social worker's initiative, without a direct request from a client. There are likely to be wide variations in the extent to which social workers translate the presentation of material problems by clients into 'applications' for money payments. Even when requests for money are presented by social workers to senior staff there is not necessarily consistency in their treatment, particularly when more than one team leader may be involved. For example one team leader pointed out:

> There is also a very different style on duty, which created considerable chaos about five weeks ago when the Area Officer and I had taken a very firm stand on a particular woman and told her she wasn't going to get as much as tuppence ha'penny from us. The next day when neither of us was on duty the duty officer made a payment.

SOCIAL WORKERS' ATTITUDES TO MONEY POWERS

The evidence cited in this section derives almost solely from the study of the social work task. The detailed study of Section 1, while collecting thorough information on payments made, did not include interviews designed to explore social workers' attitudes to their powers.

A large number of the social workers who were interviewed were generally satisfied with the scope they possessed for securing money payments for their clients, and with the mechanisms that existed to limit and control those powers. Interestingly a number of people made it very clear that they welcomed the tight hierarchical controls. Hence one qualified worker, in one of the authorities where control was very tight, argued that if they were any looser '... there would be a tendency for social workers to flash their money about a bit too much ... We have a lot of fairly inexperienced people who possibly feel terribly sympathetic towards a particular kind and would, you know, be overgenerous with the supply of money and the like.'

Another team leader in one of the authorities where social workers made quite heavy use of Section 1 expressed her view of the need for control in terms derived more from a 'social work' perspective:

> I think [it was] being brought up in the old tradition about giving money in the social work context. You know, how they used to train us, and you always had to see it as part of the goal and so on, and you had to be careful not to take away clients' independence and so on. Not to encourage dependency, all this stuff which doesn't seem to be playing such a large part in the training courses any longer ... But what gratifies me ... is that as social workers remain longer in the department you begin to see them becoming more discriminating as time goes on in their use of money. I think it's quite a heady experience for some of them initially, to be able to write off people's electricity bills, and this sort of thing, it gives them a sense of power too.

While in some ways this attitude may be seen as an example of the social work posture, criticised by Handler and Jordan, which sees money as a 'weapon' in a relationship, from another perspective this team leader was repudiating the easy assumption of 'power' by social workers. Another respondent further turned Jordan's argument on its head by suggesting that tight control over the use of money got social workers out of a situation in which they found it hard to say 'no' in a relationship with clients: ' "I'll go ahead with your application but you must understand that I can't guarantee anything" is one of the stock defences of the social worker isn't it, because you are not in fact denying the client yourself and therefore not damaging your relationship.'

As there was a lack of criticism of the restrictions on money payments, contrasting strongly with the many criticisms of authorities for failures to provide other resources, and a number of defences of the *status quo* based upon reservations about indiscriminate use of cash in social work, it is not surprising to find that many social workers were unhappy about the extent to which

they were faced by demands for, or needs for, money payments.
What is interesting about the views of those who were unhappy
about this problem is that their arguments against widespread
payments ranged from the 'tough' standpoint that clients should
'stand on their own feet' to radical arguments against social
services' discretion on grounds of equity. Linked with, or falling
between, these two kinds of arguments was a range of views that
income maintenance work and social work got in each other's way
or were incompatible.

The following are examples of what may be called the 'tough'
standpoint:

> Sometimes it's far better for the clients to sit back and think
> 'Well, how did I get into this mess, what can I do about it?', and
> perhaps to take advice from the social worker, but to learn the
> lesson the hard way rather than for the lesson not to be learnt
> and for them to get into the same trap again.

> We had a number of families who use to get into difficulties week
> in, week out, and say 'There's always the welfare'. In the old
> days they always did give them money and we found ourselves in
> the position where we had to say to people 'I'm sorry, you've got
> family allowances on Tuesday, I know this is only Friday but
> you'll have to manage'.

> I tend to be looking for people to sort out their own problem
> rather than me having to come and use resources.

In many of the areas studied, relationships with the SBC offices
were described as fairly good. Social workers did not complain
about pressure upon *them* from neglect by Supplementary Benefits.
However, elsewhere this theme did enter into social workers'
comment on money payments. In a London borough one team had
become very concerned about the number of occasions on which
they had to make payments when they felt these should have come
from the SBC. They had tried unsuccessfully to monitor their own
work. They also wrote a brusque open letter to 'All Staff' at their
local DHSS office about these grievances. Similarly in one Scottish
authority a social worker argued:

> for so long we have accepted responsibility for them. We have,
> without question, provided things which we should never have
> provided in the past, and over the years, social security, quite
> naturally, were prepared to sit back and let us do these things and
> are very loath to become involved in the work of providing what,
> in fact, statute has laid down they should provide.

This issue will be discussed fully in the next chapter.

It may be argued that some of the anger against the SBC derived simply from a reluctance to do extra work, to take on what was seen as somebody else's job. Therefore much that is said here needs to be put into context by relating it to what will be said below about the impact of financial help upon social work. But in addition it must be borne in mind that some social workers were concerned about the inadequacies and inconsistencies in their own responses to material need. Some pointed out that the SBC might well be seen by clients as 'more fair' and that: 'It's hard for clients because Section 1 is used so broadly and they will see neighbours get help with gas or electricity bills, and it's hard for them to understand whether or not it's right.'

One of the team leaders in Scotland expressed concern over the way Section 12 was often spent. He wondered how many people who had been given cash payments had found it necessary to return to the department for further help. He also thought that the general public tended to regard the social work department in a similar light to the SBC, and that it was almost impossible for them to understand the motivation behind cash payments made under Section 12. Another Scottish social worker, making a similar point, also drew attention to social workers' lack of skill in dealing with these issues. She argued: 'I feel I have no training to deal with handing out money and I don't wish to be involved in budgeting and so on.'

The very high pressure of material problems upon Scottish urban authorities and the way in which conflicts with other aspects of social work arose were well expressed by one social worker:

> I don't like having to get all panicky about things like electricity bills or rent arrears and it's fine to say they are just the sort of presenting problems and there's all sorts of things underneath, but sometimes the folk could come in with electricity bills and be not the least interested in social work. They don't want help with their other problems anyway, they just want financial help and they won't accept anything else even though you try to get in under pretext of helping with an electricity bill. I found myself one day on duty and there was a young girl in—she'd very serious marital problems and I was almost going to say 'I don't think we really could help you' and I suddenly thought, my goodness, that's what we're here for, we're not here for electricity bills. And I began to think to myself that's not going to be treated as a priority so I'd better not build up her hopes

because there's nothing really going wrong at the moment you know. Which was entirely the wrong way to look at it because that was a sort of case we should have been involved in at that point before it got any worse.

This is broadly the view that the dispensation of money, together ith other forms of help with material problems, confuses social work objectives. It was voiced by a number of respondents. Others saw such work as more explicitly distorting social work practice. According to the area officer in the Scottish area which had set up the special Section 12 committee, they had done so

because we were very alarmed at the amount we were spending and the fact that the financial dependency was becoming a real classic problem as much as the classic emotional dependency ... and we had to do something. We had to be a lot more strict over why we gave money, whom we gave it to, loan or grant, what sort of back up in terms of casework support should follow it ...

The following are some other examples of social workers expressing anxiety about the way they integrated, or failed to integrate, casework with attention to financial problems:

The more resources are the more you tend to take the easy way out ... when things are tightened up it makes you explore things more with the clients.

I don't want discretion over money—it's too open to abuse— all you do is buy time and postpone the problem.

Many social workers expressed, quite bluntly, a reluctance to handle money issues, a feeling of uncertainty when faced by problems of this kind so that they did not feel they had any basis for rational decision making:

I hate having to be faced with the choice of giving money to someone. Since I came here I haven't given money to anybody, which you know frightens me. Maybe my attitude is affecting what normally social workers would be giving out ... but I always sort of look at it as a last resort. I feel it's much better if you can find another way round it.

Perhaps the last word should come from a hospital social worker who, when asked whether she would like to share with the area teams some direct involvement in the allocation of Section 12 funds, said she 'rejoiced' in the present arrangement as she had found giving or lending money 'highly detrimental' to relationships with clients.

CHARITABLE MONEY

Many hospital social workers have access to a source of money denied to many of their area colleagues. This is money from charitable hospital funds, from which some are able to draw with a minimum of 'bureaucratic' checks. In area teams, by contrast, money from charitable sources is rarely directly given out by social workers. Rather, in a variety of situations, social workers may persuade charitable agencies to meet particular client needs. Such arrangements are generally fairly haphazard.

The situation with regard to hospital funds is varied. In the large district hospital we studied in an English county, each social worker had discretion to pay out up to £10. An administrative officer was responsible for sums over £10 but there was no expectation that social workers' requests would be refused. This situation contrasted very strongly with the restrictive rules about the use of Section 1 in the same authority, particularly for the hospital social workers who had to apply to the local area directors. Money seemed to be taken from the funds with only cursory consideration of the alternatives available. Fares to help relatives to visit the hospital were regularly paid, and on many matters the general philosophy was: 'If it's going to be a long-term thing then we would refer to social security, but if it's just a sort of one-off thing that maybe doesn't come to very much, then we would use the fund.'

In the other general hospital in this authority the fund was under the control of the welfare committee of the League of Friends. Social workers could spend up to £5 and were trying to have the figure raised to £10. If they wished to spend more they had difficulty as they had to put the case to the committee: 'They have phases when they decide they will have an economy drive and yet there will be other phases six months later when we're told we're not using the welfare fund.' Social workers complained:

They have different moral standards, different criteria for helping people ... and I have always objected to having to appeal to them. If I feel from my professional standpoint that this person needs financial help it irks me to have to go to the committee ... and sometimes they will only give half of what I've requested.

In the psychiatric hospital in the same authority very little charitable money was available. The fund had been used quite often in the past to help patients who needed, for example, fares to go for interviews for jobs. Now the fund was 'almost bankrupt'.

In the Scottish hospitals there were quite large 'comforts' and 'samaritan funds' which were 'topped up' by the health authorities. Social workers were allowed direct access to these funds and used them for fares and for small loans to patients. Here the social workers also made quite extensive use of the various societies which exist to concern themselves with the care of patients with various diseases (cancer, heart conditions, and so on).

CONCLUSIONS

This chapter has demonstrated some of the primary sources of variation in the use of grant-giving powers by social workers, both by the use of statistical information on the character of those variations and by the exploration of departmental policies and social workers' attitudes. The discussion has suggested a number of problems which may be seen as deserving of attention: the extent of the variations in the use of money, the implications of policies on the giving of loans, the impact of money giving upon social work and the underlying difficulties produced by the policies of other agencies. Some solutions to these will be discussed in Chapter 4. It would be premature to start on a fuller consideration of any single issue until the full range of issues, complications and implications have been given attention. Hence the next chapter adds a crucial piece to the picture by looking at relations between social workers and the SBC both on the money payment issue and on the broader range of clients' material problems.

Chapter 3

Social Work and Supplementary Benefits

INTRODUCTION

The most significant contribution to the discussion of the relationship between social work and the administration of the supplementary benefits scheme is Olive Stevenson's book *Claimant or Client?* She is there concerned to talk to both sides and to stress the need for an effective and constructive relationship. She was writing on the basis of her experience of secondment for eighteen months as the first Social Work Adviser to the Supplementary Benefits Commission. During her time with the SBC she had been involved, amongst other things, in trying to foster this relationship between the two services. One of her recommendations to the SBC was that they should set up a permanent team of social work advisers. This was accepted. She also did a great deal to stimulate ways of increasing understanding between local SBC staff and field workers in social services departments—through meetings, secondment schemes, and so on.

A central theme of Olive Stevenson's book is that while the separation of income maintenance and social work is an important and desirable feature of the British welfare system, nevertheless a recognition of the 'whole man', of the fundamental links between the meeting of material need and the meeting of psychological and emotional needs, is 'essential to the administration of creative justice'. She argues (1973, p. 36):

> On the one hand, it is absolutely clear ... that the problems of some individuals are so intertwined as to make a total separation of financial from other social services not only impractical but undesirable if their welfare is to be genuinely safeguarded. On the other hand, the control of various aspects of an individual's life via the provision of money must be subject to stringent limitations and careful scrutiny. This does not necessarily mean, however, that it is always improper but that there must be certain

safeguards, of which the two most important are: first, that entitlements to basic allowances cannot rest or be believed to rest by claimants, on compliance with what is considered socially desirable behaviour (such as sending the children to school). If there is any 'bargaining' of this kind, it should be in relation to extras. Secondly, the nature of these bargains should be much more clearly understood by workers (in this case officials or social workers) and by the clients themselves, so that the implications of the control being exercised are more honestly examined.

A central concern of this book is to look at the issues of balance raised by Olive Stevenson. What is the implication of the growth of money payments for the relationship between social work and income maintenance? To what extent is provision for 'extras' becoming a social services' responsibility? How do social workers relate to the SBC in situations in which they may themselves be the providers of benefits, be assisting the SBC in what are broadly 'social control' activities, or be operating as advisers and advocates on behalf of clients seeking to obtain more help from the SBC?

In the first half of this chapter, the discussion of money payments in the last chapter will be continued by looking at the issues these raise about the social services/SBC interface. In this discussion the main supportive material will be derived from our study of Section 1 payments in six English authorities. Then in the second part some of the broader aspects of social services/SBC relationships will be examined. Here the main sources will be the study of the social work task. It is important to point out that both of the research sources used present a one-sided picture of relationships. Neither study included interviews of SBC staff to see how they regarded the issues discussed. While this is obviously in some respects a weakness, the purpose of this book is to explore the implications of money problems for the social work task and not to analyse in depth the role played by the SBC on these issues. There is in progress, at the time of writing, a study of these issues which involves interviews on 'both sides of the fence'. This is based at Manchester University. It is hoped that it will in due course make a valuable contribution to the exploration of the topics covered in this book.

MONEY PAYMENTS AND SUPPLEMENTARY BENEFITS

In recent years increasing evidence has been produced on the payment of Section 1, or in Scotland Section 12, money to people also on supplementary benefits. Much of this evidence is cited in Lister and Emmett's pamphlet *Under the Safety Net* (1976). While there are marked variations from place to place it would appear that up to about half of all payments go to families who are also on supplementary benefits. The other studies also suggest, as does the evidence cited in the last chapter, that a high proportion of these payments is for needs which the supplementary benefits scheme is designed to cover. Lister and Emmett draw two implications: that the SBC is not fully meeting its responsibilities, and that social workers are not doing enough to ensure that the maximum help is obtained from supplementary benefits before Section 1 payments are made.

The SBC has given considerable attention to this problem, and in September 1976 a revised version of a memorandum jointly produced by the SBC and the local authority associations, 'Assistance in cash', made an attempt to clarify the situation. However, at the core of the problem, as both the SBC and its critics recognise, is the fact that overlap occurs at the point where discretionary powers to deal with exceptional situations meet from both sides. The point was well made from the SBC's point of view in the chairman's response to *Under the Safety Net* (Donnison, 1976):

There are legislative limitations, both explicit and implicit, on the way we exercise our functions. An example of the explicit is the use of the words 'exceptional' and 'urgent' in Section 7 and 13 respectively of the 1966 Act; and of the implicit, the fact that the scale rates are fixed by Parliament at levels intended to cover all normal expenses other than housing costs. In using our discretionary powers to vary the statutory provisions we must have regard to these limitations as well as to the requirement to 'promote the welfare' of the people with whom we deal: this compels us to make judgements about what constitutes an exceptional or urgent need, and to refrain from making discretionary payments in such a way as, effectively, to substitute our own judgement for that of Parliament about the adequacy of the scale rates. If we *constantly* pay extra benefits to those who manage their affairs badly we will so alienate others—

claimants and non-claimants—that the scheme itself will be destroyed, and our discretionary powers with it.

The local authorities have not produced a comparably powerful spokesman to put a similar case from their point of view. However, in this clash of institutional powers claimants and clients are in the middle; perhaps suffering from the ambiguities of the situation, perhaps gaining because of the possibility of going to two places for help. The study of the use of Section 1 in England was particularly designed to throw light on this issue.

Table 3.1 shows, for the six English authorities studied, the numbers who were in receipt of supplementary benefits at the time the Section 1 payment was made. It also includes two other figures, the numbers on supplementary benefits at any time in the six months prior to, and the one month after, their payment, and the numbers who were on supplementary benefits throughout this period. These additional figures show that a high proportion of Section 1 payment recipients were liable to need supplementary benefits from time to time while a comparatively low proportion were continuously dependent on this source of income. The variations between the three figures help to demonstrate one of the difficulties about developing coherent policies to meet the needs of this group of people, so many of whom experience frequently changing circumstances.

Table 3.1 *Supplementary benefit experience of Section 1 recipient by authority (the figures in brackets are percentages of the total Section 1 recipients in each area)*

	All 6	Midlands Borough	Northern Borough 1	London Borough	Southern County	Northern County	Northern Borough 2
On SB at time of payment	168 (39)	27 (38)	49 (48)	9 (41)	12 (34)	43 (28)	28 (55)
On SB throughout 7 months	97 (22)	11 (16)	24 (24)	5 (23)	8 (23)	27 (18)	22 (43)
On SB at any time in 7 months	221 (51)	43 (61)	50 (49)	19 (54)	19 (54)	63 (42)	37 (73)

With the data available it is hard to explain the variations from area to area shown Table 3.1. The authorities with the highest proportions on supplementary benefits at the time of payment were the two northern boroughs. In the case of Northern Borough 2 this seems explicable in terms of a greater tendency for its clients to be on supplementary benefits at any time. This authority probably had the highest unemployment rate of the six areas studied, though it must be emphasised that it was not an area of major unemployment.

Table 3.2 is concerned with the extent to which there were variations in the purposes for which Section 1 payments were made between people receiving or not receiving supplementary benefits. In the case of grants for clothing the position was as might be expected: payments were typically made to people not on supplementary benefits. The position with regard to day care might have been expected to be the other way round since SBC help is not normally available for this. However, perhaps the low figure for those on supplementary benefits is explained by the extent to which day care payments were used to help working parents. Apart from these two cases, which involve relatively small numbers of payments, it is surprising that the proportions on supplementary benefits were so close to the aggregate proportion. In particular, it is worthy of comment that payments for food and fuel were made to so may people who were in receipt of supplementary benefits.

Of the payments to supplementary benefits recipients, 69 per cent were under £5, as opposed to 45 per cent of the payments to

Table 3.2 *Purposes of Section 1 payments to supplementary benefits recipients*

Purpose of payment	Number of SB recipients getting such payment	SB recipients as a percentage of all getting payments for this purpose
All purposes	168	39
Appliances	12	40
Food	81	42
Clothing	4	22
Fuel	30	41
Day Care	9	29
Transport	11	42
Accommodation	10	38

other people. This difference is partly explained by the importance of food payments to supplementary benefits recipients.

Social workers were as ready to make loans to supplementary benefits recipients as to anyone else: 33 per cent of the payments overall were loans and 32 per cent of the payments to supplementary benefits recipients were loans. Since, as will be shown, social workers were often mistaken as to whether their client was on supplementary benefits, perhaps a more significant statistic is the fact that 35 per cent of payments to people whom social workers *thought were on* supplementary benefits were loans.

In 194 cases (45 per cent) social workers said they had approached the SBC to see if they could meet the need. It is important to qualify this statistic, and some of the other ones on dealings with the SBC, with the note that records were often unsatisfactory so that the answer to this question therefore depended on a combination of consultation of records and recall by the social worker. SBC records showed much lower figures for contacts of this kind, but since most of the exchanges were by telephone it is probable that SBC staff rarely noted such conversations. (As far as their side of the exchange was concerned the research was entirely dependent upon the existence of a written record.)

Table 3.3 further amplifies the information about approaches by social workers to the SBC by relating those to whether or not people were on supplementary benefits.

Table 3.3 *Whether SBC approached for help by whether family actually on SB (percentages of numbers on or not on SB in brackets)*

Actually on SB	SB Approached		
	Yes	No	D.K.
Yes	92 (55)	67 (40)	8 (5)
No	102 (38)	149 (56)	14 (5)

Social workers thought that many more people were receiving supplementary benefits than was actually the case. In 108 cases social workers thought people were in receipt when they were not, and in 25 they thought they were not when in fact they were. They were therefore wrong in about a third of all the cases in the samples.

It might have been expected that this discrepancy would have been the other way round, that social workers were making Section 1 payments to people on the mistaken and unverified assumption that they were not on supplementary benefits. However, this curious finding is indicative of a general lack of care taken by social workers in checking the material circumstances of those who come to them for help. They would seem to be likely to be nearly as confused as the general public about the distinction between supplementary benefits and any other kinds of benefits, probably frequently misled by their clients' confusion about their benefits, or at least thoroughly muddled by their clients' varying dependence on different sources of income.

There was comparatively little variation between the authorities in readiness to approach the SBC to see if they would pay, except that in the particularly 'welfare rights conscious' Northern Borough 1 approaches were made in 69 per cent of the cases. This can be contrasted with the figure of 45 per cent overall. However, approaches were most commonly made where food grants were being considered, in 61 per cent of the cases, and Northern Borough 1 made a particularly large number of such payments. It would have been illuminating to study all situations in which clients asked for Section 1 payments so that situations in which the SBC made payments instead, or payments were refused, were taken into account, but the lack of written records of such events precluded further research.

Next to food payments, fuel payments figured most prominently amongst situations in which SBC help was sought. In 53 per cent of the cases involving fuel debts the SBC was approached for this purpose. These two kinds of payments are, of course, those for which social workers might particularly be expected to seek SBC help. It is perhaps more important to emphasise the negative point that in *only* 53 per cent of these was the SBC approached. Furthermore, in 30 per cent of the cases where food payments were being made to people actually on SB no approach was made. Similarly in 45 per cent of the situations where fuel payments were being considered the SBC was not approached, and again the figure was 30 per cent for people actually on benefits.

Since social workers rarely made the mistake of assuming their clients were not on supplementary benefits when in fact they were, obviously they rarely failed to contact the SBC simply because they took it that their clients were not known. Hence the numbers of cases where clients could directly exploit the social services' ignorance in this way were very limited. There were a few examples of this kind, however. For example, in two very similar cases, clients secured £3 Section 1 payments on the grounds that they were starting work and waiting for a 'week in hand' when they had received full payments from the SBC for the same purpose. The social workers had said that the SBC was not approached because their clients were not in receipt of benefit.

In the survey an attempt was made to find out why Section 1 decisions had been made in some cases without consultation with the SBC. In general the replies reflected social workers' assumptions about their clients' eligibility for such help. In 35 per cent of the cases the social workers said their clients were not eligible for SBC help and in 23 per cent they said the need was not of a kind which the SBC could be expected to meet. Unfortunately in 29 per cent of cases social workers were unable to recall by the time of interview why such an approach had not been made. The other reasons for failing to contact the SBC were few. In some cases social workers regarded their payments as explicitly furthering a casework relationship (1 per cent of cases). In some others, the fact that the DHSS offices were closed was given as the reason for not making contact (5 per cent), while occasionally there was understood to be an explicit 'deal' under which the problems were to be dealt with by social services (3 per cent). Finally in 5 per cent of the cases no approach was made because social workers felt that the SBC response to their particular client would be unsympathetic.

In discussions social work staff, both in the 'six authorities survey' and in the wider study of the social work task, raised a variety of further points about the feasibility of approaching supplementary benefits for help. In some places social work area offices were a very long way from the nearest SBC offices. The consequence was that Section 1 payments for food were made because it was seen as hopeless to send clients on 10- to 15-mile journeys, or Section 1 payments were made for fares to enable clients to reach SBC offices. Such decisions may reflect a failure to explore adequately the scope for an arrangement with local offices to enable social services to make payments which could be recovered from the SBC. These cases were similar to those where Section 1 payments were made to meet emergencies arising when SBC offices were closed.

It was reported above that in 194 cases the SBC was approached by social workers. In a small number of these the SBC agreed to meet part of the need—in all, about eight cases. In the remaining 186 help was refused. However, what must be emphasised is that, since this was a study of Section 1 *payments,* there is no way of knowing on how many other occasions the use of Section 1 may have been considered but in fact SBC offices agreed to meet the need.

Naturally, also, in a good many situations where SBC help was refused the client was not known to be, or was not, at that time on benefit. While in some of those it may be argued that emergency payments might have been made by the SBC, the lack of information available from the research makes such a judgement impossible. Accordingly attention must be focused upon the ninety-two cases where the client was actually on supplementary benefits.

In fifty-two cases the application was for a payment for food. In fourteen of these this was refused by the SBC on the ground that the payment was already in the post. These included situations where Giros were lost or delayed. A particular difficulty here might be that SBC were suspicious of a claim that a Giro was lost. For example, in one such case the client claimed to have lost a Giro on four other occasions in the preceding six months, and each time the Giro had been cashed. This was information given subsequently to the researchers. It is not known what social services were told. This was an extreme example of a problem reported in several cases. On the other hand, in another situation which was examined social services were told that some Giros had been destroyed as a result of flooding at the DHSS offices. It seems surprising that the SBC did not pay again in this situation. In twenty-one of these fifty-two cases SBC help was refused on the grounds that it had already been given. These were cases where clients said they were unable to manage on the basic allowances. Some of the most difficult examples of this kind were those which arose when the male partner in a family was only an intermittent member of the household. In a further fourteen cases the reason for SBC refusal was unclear. In three, according to the social workers, the client was not on supplementary benefits. They were presumably misinformed.

In twenty cases the Section 1 payments were for help with fuel bills, and in a further seven they were for appliances (generally, calor gas cookers supplied to people with fuel debt problems). These twenty-seven can therefore be taken together. Seven of the eight examples of payment sharing between the two departments came under this category. A good example of this was a case where Section 1 money was used to purchase a gas cooker from a charity and the SBC paid for its installation. But there were others where, although explicit sharing arrangements did not appear to have been made, nevertheless the two departments were both contributing to the solution of the same problem. For example, in one situation where the SBC had paid the electricity bill the re-connection charge was paid by social services. The SBC was not approached to see if it would meet this; the social worker felt that it had given so much help towards fuel bills in the recent past that it was not reasonable to ask for this further help

In thirteen of these twenty-seven cases social workers were told that supplementary benefits were not available for this purpose or that payment for this had been made (since duplication of payments did not ensue, this may be taken to be a reference to the provision for fuel costs in the basic allowance). In two cases Section 1 money was used to pay fuel debts after supplementary benefits appeal tribunals had endorsed refusal of a grant for that purpose. In another case, similar help was given after the client had sought SBC help and been informed that help would be considered if she agreed to voluntary deductions for future fuel bills. She angrily refused to have deductions made.

In two other situations SBC help was refused when it was understood that 'cohabitees' had broken into gas meters. Here the social worker agreed that the SBC was right to refuse but a Section 1 payment was made nevertheless. Some of the reasons for the complications which arise over fuel debts are explored in the Appendix. Three of the cases of refusal were concerned with transport costs and five with accommodation. There were five other refusals. The numbers involved here were too small to justify further examination.

Two general points emerge from the analysis in the last two paragraphs: (1) the considerable number of situations in which the SBC felt that it had done all that was required of it as far as 'food' payment applications were concerned, and also to a lesser extent in the case of fuel needs; and (2) the sharing arrangements made in relation to some fuel debts.

In ten cases social services recovered some money from the SBC and in a further three clients repaid money on receipt of supplementary benefits. The memorandum 'Assistance in cash' discusses the need for reimbursement arrangements, particularly when emergencies arise outside normal SBC office hours. The impression from the social work task research is that such arrangements were patchy, working much better in some areas than others. Many social workers resented acting as agents for the SBC in this way, particularly when emergencies arose not in the middle of the night, but, for example, at times when SBC offices were closed but staff had not yet finished work.

In only seven cases was the refusal of SBC help given in writing. In over two-thirds of the cases where the SBC was approached the social worker was told, presumably usually over the telephone, that help could not be given. Only very rarely, too, did the client negotiate directly with the SBC. In seven cases the client was the source of the information that the SBC could not help. Hence, there existed a decision-making process that was seldom formalised. Social workers were being told that no help could be given in circumstances in which they had little information as to how thoroughly the SBC had considered the case, and in which they often did not know whether there had been a formal decision or whether their informant was the person who had made, or might make, that decision.

The emphasis in the discussion of overlap between the two departments has been upon requests for Section 1 payments when, in the SBC's view, the need had already been met through the basic allowance. However, it was possible also to relate Section 1 payments to SBC exceptional need payments (ENPs). This investigation did not uncover examples of ENPs and Section 1 payments being made at the same time to meet the same need. However, there was a limited number of examples—though insufficient to justify precise analysis—of payment of Section 1 money to meet fuel debts when ENPs had been made for the same reason to meet earlier bills.

Nevertheless, the striking finding from this part of the data analysis was the very high proportion of the people on supplementary benefits who had received ENPs within the time studied (that is, six months before their payment and one month after): 136 families had received ENPs, that is, 62 per cent of the number in the sample who were on supplementary benefits *at any time* within the seven months. Furthermore, 57 of that 136, that is, 42 per cent, received more than one ENP within the period. Details were only kept of up to three ENPs but in a few cases there were several. For example, one family had six, in the period studied, for a variety of purposes: food, blankets, and large sums for fuel bills. Manifestly, therefore, the people who come to social services for 'exceptional payments' are likely to have received 'exceptional' help from the SBC too. However, that help is unlikely to have been for the same purpose as the Section 1 payment. Only 18 per cent of the ENPs were for fuel, while 37 per cent were for clothing and 23 per cent for furniture, two needs which were rarely met from Section 1. This leaves 21 per cent given for other purposes of varying kinds - though in some of these cases the purpose of the payment had not been recorded.

It is difficult to relate this data on numbers of exceptional needs payments to what is known about the overall frequency of such payments by the SBC. But some comparison is necessary to justify the use of the word 'striking' in the previous paragraph. According to the 1976 annual report of the SBC, 17 per cent of the 2.8 million recipients of regular weekly supplementary pensions and allowances in December 1975 had received one or more ENPs during the previous twelve months. However, the report also shows that unemployed claimants and single parents were much more likely to receive ENPs than supplementary pensioners, hence a direct comparison between our 62 per cent and this figure of 17 per cent would be misleading. Sixteen per cent of unemployed claimants had received one or more ENP, and 48 per cent of single parents had done so. These are the two groups most likely to be included in the sample of recipients of Section 1 payments. Over half of all ENPs were for clothing or footwear, a little over 10 per cent were for bedding and a similar percentage were for furniture. Just under 10 per cent were for fuel.

This discussion of Section 1 has suggested a measure of overlap between the responsibilities of the SBC and commitments undertaken by social services departments. Unless the view is taken that the SBC should meet a very much wider range of exceptional needs. including those of many people not in receipt of a weekly allowance, it must be stressed that it is an overlap 'at the margins' and not involving at least half of those granted Section 1 payments. More over the study does not suggest in any conclusive way where the blame may lie for the overlap, or indeed whether or not 'blame' is an appropriate word to use. In some cases the SBC seemed to have refused payment in circumstances in which it might have been reasonable for it to make one. But we were not often able to obtain an account of its reasons for refusing. Rather more frequently social workers seemed to have made payments without either effectively checking with the SBC or attempting to press it to examine or re-examine its decision. But we were collecting accounts of behaviour some time after decisions were taken, and we cannot be sure that social workers were wrong in assuming that clients had obtained all they could from the SBC. What was produced, therefore, was an account of one aspect of relationships between the two agencies, an aspect that must tend to confuse clients perhaps already far from clear about the distinction between social services and social security. Social services staff were meeting needs which are regularly met, for other people (including other clients), by the SBC. While social services rarely met clothing needs with cash payments and, we may safely assume, the SBC rarely paid for holidays or day care, the majority of Section 1 payments were for needs—food, fuel debts and fares—that were also regularly met by the SBC.

Social workers were certainly frequently concerned about their roles as the providers of benefits which might have been given by the SBC. Both this chapter and the previous one have quoted some evidence of this disquiet. Our research is not alone in citing evidence on this topic. Indeed, within social work, concern about it has been sufficiently widespread for the British Association of Social Workers (BASW) to draw up a 'cash code' in an attempt to limit the use of Section 1. In this they particularly emphasise the case against making payments to clients eligible for SBC help, and urge the full use of appeal procedures in those circumstances.

Clearly Section 1 poses very special problems for the relationship between social workers and the SBC, and the issue of the link between direct cash aid and social work is an important one. But social workers are asked by their clients for help with material problems in very many situations in which cash payments from social services' funds are not, indeed sometimes cannot, be considered. There is a need now, therefore, to place this issue in the broader context of relationships between the two agencies in general.

RELATIONSHIPS BETWEEN SOCIAL WORKERS AND SUPPLEMENTARY BENEFITS: SOME GENERAL CONSIDERATIONS

Contrary to the impression widely provided by the social work press, and contrary to that likely to be gained from an intensive consideration of the money payments problem, our interviews of social workers, conducted as part of the social work task research, did not suggest that relationships between social services and the SBC were generally bad. The main examples of bad relationships came from the places where they might be most expected, the areas of high stress for clients and for staff in both agencies; while from the quieter areas, and particularly from the rural areas, came many accounts of good working relationships. Such 'good relationships' have a great deal to do with the personalities and attitudes of staff on either side. Moreover, to say that two departments had 'good relationships' should not be taken to mean either that one agency always did what the other wanted, or that the outcome of this relationship was necessarily beneficial to the clients.

An accommodation between two agencies based upon mutual understanding of each other's policies and problems, and upon good manners on either side, does not, in itself, rule out substantial areas of disagreement. Thus, for example, one social worker said of the SBC staff: 'They are very helpful until it comes to parting with the money.' Furthermore, the fact that many social workers expressed satisfaction with the role played by the SBC may tell us as much about the attitudes of the social workers as it does about the policies and behaviour of staff from the other agency. In this section some of the comments may help to correct the stereotype of social workers, held, it is suspected, by many social security staff, as militants at war with the other agencies of the welfare state and ready to put their clients' material needs before any other considerations.

The reported relationship with the SBC in the English and Welsh counties studied, most of the Irish teams apart from the 'intake team' in the Border area, a borough in the North of England, and some of the teams in Scotland, was generally good. The main groups to express strong discontent with the SBC were the social workers in London, those in the urban stress area covered by one of the Scottish authorities and those in the Irish intake team. A very mixed picture was presented by social workers from another Scottish region. The hospital social workers studied tended to have little contact with the SBC. In almost every team, however, there were individuals who viewed the SBC rather differently from their colleagues, and who might resent these generalisations. Perspectives on the SBC are significantly influenced by political views about the welfare state and the role of social work within it.

One further important general point must be stressed. Many social workers said that relationships between the two departments had improved markedly in the immediate past. In doing so they paid tribute to the various liaison arrangements and interdepartmental visits and exchanges that had been developed. The following statement by a team leader is quoted at length because it sets out well a number of aspects of the relationship between the agencies, stresses the improvements made and expresses a view about the scope for further progress:

> things are improving. At one time on the social worker level it was very bad. I think the blame must be attributed to the social workers in some respects, inasmuch as we had one or two who

got rather hoit-toity and thought that because they were qualified
social workers they were above everybody else. They used to
adopt a rather patronising tone and I think that supplementary
benefits felt that these social workers were trying to teach
their grannies how to suck eggs, so to speak. For a time relations
were not very good at all ... but ... they seem to me to be
improved, and, certainly, if I've gone down to supplementary
benefits with a client I've been treated with the utmost courtesy.
There are one or two officers in supplementary benefits that are
not easy to deal with in an amicable way, but I could imagine
they could say the same about us. But, obviously, the people up
above are anxious that we should have a good working
relationship and, to this end, we went down in teams and actually
met the supplementary benefits people. To me, I don't think that
one meeting is of very much value. I would have liked to see
follow-up visits, even if it was only a visit every three months.
Once you get to know a person's face and you remember their
name and you see them on occasions, I think this makes for a
better working relationship between you ... In the main
relationships are quite good.

In one of the boards in Northern Ireland, where relations were
generally good, both districts had run schemes to enable team
members to spend several days in SBC offices as observers.
Everyone who had experienced this scheme said it had been
valuable. They now had a clearer idea of the problems faced by
their counterparts and communications had improved. In another
authority SBC staff had spent two days with the duty officer in one
of the social work teams. There were also frequent meetings
between senior social services staff and DHSS management. Many
social workers had been able to get to know SBC visiting officers
personally.

Even in the Scottish area where there were many problems social
workers paid tribute to the progress which had been made with
liaison arrangements. They particularly praised the efforts made by
their divisional director during the past year in developing
discussions:

> it's incredible the movement in DHSS ... I don't think the social
> work department ... ever really spoke to DHSS before and it's
> amazing in a year what's happened.

It is perhaps unfortunate that one area attributed improvements
in relationships to their management, while the other blamed

changes in DHSS management for deterioration. It is perhaps natural that things are seen in this way. However the general points being made about management on both sides are important.

The two urban areas in which relations were acknowledged to be bad were both inner city areas where clients faced considerable problems of poverty and poor housing. They were also areas where both departments were under heavy pressure not only because of these problems but also because of the extra work created by population movements, shifts of people in and out of work, one-parent families and people with unstable ways of life. They were also perhaps areas where the staff in both departments changed rapidly. In the last sense they differed from the other very deprived area studied, the borough in Northern England, which was generally more stable. This may partly explain why social services/SBC relations were said to be much better in that area. Significantly the other place where particularly difficult relationships were reported was in an Irish town close to the Border, and seriously disturbed by the 'troubles', where again some of the features listed above were present.

This argument that it may be problems of change in a context of deprivation rather than merely the latter which makes for difficult relationships is further supported by evidence on the extent to which social security problems for social workers were primarily 'duty' or 'intake' problems. This may partly explain the distinction drawn between the 'turbulent' relations with the SBC reported by the 'intake team' in Northern Ireland and the less fraught situation for the 'long-term' team serving parts of the same district. One of the social workers from a Scottish team where duty work was shared drew this same contrast from his own experience:

> On intake you ... [have a lot to do with them] but not in the normal run of the mill; and again I suppose your contact is a bit different when it's in relation to clients that you do know, and you're supporting them to make claims for exceptional needs payments ... On intake, kinds of situations that create problems are people who have appeared in ... [the city] for the first time, for instance, and aren't known to the DHSS office, or are making requests for an emergency payment ... Whereas the clients we know are also known over a period of time, usually to that office and therefore there is a file on them ... So that when you send a letter they usually can deal with it, and then there is not the same urgency.

This is an important observation with implications both for the organisation of duty work in some of these stress areas, and for the kinds of skills required by those who specialise in such work.

The discussion so far has centred upon the reasons why the general pattern of relationships between the two agencies was either good or bad. To provide a complete picture more attention must be given to some of the more mixed situations where social workers in the same office gave very different accounts of relationships, and where individuals themselves reported very varied experiences.

In one Scottish region where very mixed reports were given on relations with SBC, some social workers said 'It is not a running battle', 'they always seem willing to listen', 'I haven't had to hassle too much', and so on. Others described SBC officers as 'the worst to deal with', 'very condescending' and 'inconsistent', and saw contact as 'a running battle'. These differences may be largely ascribed to personalities on either side, but there were some structural features that may have made matters difficult. In one team the social work department seemed to have given little attention to liaison. 'Someone' in the divisional hierarchy was said to have this function, but as there was little contact between him and the fieldworkers this may have produced little practical benefit. Another team had to deal with a DHSS sub-office open only one and a half days a week. At other times they had to contact a rather distant office.

Several social workers, in different areas, referred to what they saw as SBC staff's prejudices about particular types of clients. Therefore, in 'difficult' areas in which social workers inevitably meet 'difficult' clients who are unpopular with SBC staff, this must further exacerbate relationships. One of the social workers in London reported that SBC officers 'have said to me "They should be working, earning their own money"', and another summed up attitudes as follows:

> There is a difference between someone who is deserving poor —you notice quite a lot of prejudice when you ring up ... if they are unemployed or unmarried mothers you get a totally different attitude than if they are elderly or disabled.

It should not go unremarked, however, that in some areas social workers had themselves expressed fairly 'tough' attitudes towards the making of money payments. Therefore, some of the social workers who expressed satisfaction with the relationship with the SBC may have shared the attitudes quoted above. Some social workers acknowledged that they operated policies on money payments—close supervision of the use of money, payments in kind, the holding of child benefit books while a loan was outstanding which did not exemplify a level of trust of clients comparable to that which others expected from the SBC. The important difference may be in readiness to express stereotypes and moral judgements.

It is perhaps most fair to end a discussion in which emphasis has been upon the varying special circumstances in which 'bad' relationships existed between social workers and SBC staff with some examples from the very many interviews with social workers in which they stressed that 'it all depends ...':

> I think it depends on the person at the other end, it depends on what it is you're asking for, it seems to depend on a lot of variables, some of which are very difficult to pinpoint like, maybe ... [the local office] are having a bad week.

> Individuals working there can bend the rules, depending on what they feel like that particular day.

> There are times when an individual officer will really put himself out to help clients. But the majority of contacts, on duty days, everyone is harassed, both at DHSS and here, and tempers get frayed. The frustration mounts and people blow their tops.

STRUCTURAL PROBLEMS IN SOCIAL WORK/SBC RELATIONSHIPS

Some of the comments made by social workers suggest that difficulties between social workers and supplementary benefits staff may be related to differences in the structures of the two departments. Several issues can be identified: the problem of the right 'level' for contacts, changes in the staff involved, lack of understanding of the ways in which each work, and, related to all of these, the problem of identification of named people.

The discovery of these issues is nothing new. They were given considerable attention by Olive Stevenson in *Claimant or Client?* and have featured in many subsequent discussions between social workers and SBC staff. In some respects the great attention that has been given to liaison arrangements, as many of the social workers testified, has helped to alleviate them. But this effort may to some extent have been undermined by the requirements of streamlined management systems in DHSS offices, the reduction in visiting and the high turnover of staff. The agencies clearly relate best in situations in which both departments are operating on broadly compatible 'patches'. Without this, argued one social worker in Northern Ireland:

> you can never figure out who you're supposed to approach. It's good if you can get to know one person—get to know their first name. You can discuss things with them and they'll get to know you.

Similarly, it was very much easier in places where staff changes were rare. As one Welsh team leader put it:

> I have worked [in this area] for about five years, and so a lot of people who were executive officers then are assistant managers now, and I knew them as people. If anyone was in difficulty they would come to me and I'd have a word with one of them and nine times out of ten get a quick reply.

In the more difficult areas, therefore, social workers stressed the importance of getting through to the right person:

> If you can get through the barrage of bureaucracy, talk humanly and trenchantly to the liaison officer [it's better].

> Once when I was very annoyed they put me through to the actual visitor. It was so different being able to talk to somebody who actually knew the family ... we could discuss it at a reasonable level.

On the social services side, too, it may be important to get known and trusted:

> they get to know they can trust you when you say 'this is rather urgent'.

A trainee expressed the value of personal contact both for establishing a relationship, and for acquiring an understanding of the SBC's perspective:

> I know that some of the social workers in the office, their names are taboo down at social security, but I have always found them to be all right. What I try to do is not only to talk to them on the telephone but to pop in and see them. Just walking in there

and seeing the amount of paper work makes me think they are not so bad after all.

That trainee worked in an authority where relationships were said to be fairly good. Interestingly, here, the social services area office had previously been in the same building as the SBC office, and some of those who had worked there attributed this good relationship to having made personal acquaintances.

Yet clearly, and perhaps largely for some of the organisational reasons outlined above, in many of the larger offices social workers did not succeed in making the personal contacts they would like. One social worker joked:

> They're very funny about giving out names ... they'd rather say 'well ask for extension 212' so you are always speaking to extensions.

Judging by the number of times social workers mentioned it, this 'names' issue seemed to be of considerable importance to them. Indeed, one social worker stressed the problem in this way:

> I think that social workers are great believers in the personal touch anyway. This was an argument we used to have with supplementary benefits ... There are so many people who work there that it is difficult to get back to the same person. We were always happy to give our name.

Because they were not given names and were not given information that would enable them to place their SBC contact in his hierarchy or in relation to his responsibilities, social workers found that they were unable to relate properly to the structure. They did not know whether they were talking to a 'go-between' or a 'decision-maker'. Their response to a frustrating interchange with an unidentifiable SBC official was to 'go up the hierarchy'. Then they were sometimes seen as offending against understandings that had been made about appropriate levels of contact. One social worker reported an example of this:

> I telephoned the area manager at DHSS and I got ripped off for it because he said 'don't you speak to me — don't you ever speak to me—your area officer can speak to me. This must be done at proper levels'!

In one area the designation of a liaison officer within the SBC seemed to have helped with this problem, in another a special welfare officer largely played this liaison role. These appeared, however, to be exceptions. Elsewhere either a range of individual contacts had been made, in some of the ways discussed above, or the situation was very muddled. In the area where the tensions seemed to be highest, the London Borough, it was said:

> We wanted to get some meaningful dialogue with them but no luck. They are disappearing further behind a bureaucratic wall.

SPECIFIC AREAS OF CONFLICT BETWEEN THE TWO AGENCIES

The discussion of money payments by social workers has already identified one of the main areas of conflict with the SBC. Central to this was the problem of claims from clients in immediate need of help for food. The most difficult frontier problem tended to arise in those areas where social services had been most ready to make payments in the past, in Scotland and in London. However, even in the areas where social services rarely made such payments they were confronted by clients who sought their help in getting money from the SBC.

A particular source of frustration when our field studies were first started was the absence in many areas of an SBC out-of-hours duty system. Since that time this issue has been settled, and duty systems would appear to be generally in operation. However, a source of annoyance to social workers was the fact that, while their own duty system required considerable restriction of their social life, the agreement between DHSS and the civil service unions does not require their duty officers to stay at home, and does not allow for the elaborate back-up system which is essential in social services departments. Accordingly social workers on out-of-hours duty did from time to time have to handle social security problems, and made payments which they hoped to be able to reclaim from the SBC. Sometimes the arrangements for reimbursement did not work well. While many social workers, particularly in places where problems of distance made it difficult for SBC staff to visit, quite readily accepted that they should occasionally make payments as agents for DHSS, others were unhappy about taking on such responsibilities.

One special issue which was of concern to social workers in the hospitals was the SBC's role in helping with the fares of relatives visiting patients. Social workers seemed very confused as to what the SBC could do in these circumstances. Some staff seemed to have little knowledge about the position at all, and tended to dip into hospital funds for this purpose. Others had tried to get SBC help, and, having failed, concluded that nothing could be done:

> They will not pay the visiting expenses of any relative visiting hospital, not unless there is a really good reason. Even with children they don't—we have tried it but they normally say you must apply to social services.

Others had been more successful:

> What I tend to do is negotiate with social security, give them the circumstances, how long the child is going to be in hospital and they are usually quite happy to pay.

Since hospital social workers may not be involved in the day-to-day 'duty' contact with the SBC it may be that they are forgotten when departmental liaison and information-giving functions are considered.

Hospital social workers tended to become more involved than their field colleagues in contributory benefit problems, because of the rules relating to application for, and payment of, sickness, invalidity and disablement benefits. However, this kind of work was often the responsibility of clerical and administrative staff. 'One tries not to do the DHSS stuff', said one social worker in a general hospital, adding that in her training 'it wasn't the done thing to handle pension books'.

At the time of writing a new issue affecting relations between the agencies is beginning to emerge which illustrates well the difficulties in getting the relationship 'right'. The DHSS is under heavy pressure from the Treasury to reduce its staffing complement. The main scope for savings lies in the labour intensive local administration of supplementary benefits. To achieve savings the SBC must cut home visiting. One of the ways of doing this is for visits to be omitted when requests are made for exceptional needs payments. Accordingly, local office staff have been instructed that when social workers send in requests for ENPs for items listed as within the normal departmental rules, for clients whose domestic circumstances they know, payments should be made without either a visit or an office interview.

On the face of it this looks like a proposal that will be welcome to social workers. Certainly, the attitudes of many social workers quoted in this and the last chapter suggest that this new rule will be acceptable. Conversations with social workers, since the research was completed indicate, however, that many are uneasy about it. The change is seen as shifting the burden of visiting and verification on to social workers. While the SBC stresses that the responsibility for the decision will remain its own, social workers fear that they will be under some pressure to ensure that they preserve their credibility with the SBC. Will they find that if they ask too often, or are subsequently proved to have misjudged situations, their recommendations will be disregarded while those from their colleagues are still accepted?

Furthermore, this proposal needs to be seen in the context of the disquiet about the growing use of Section 1. It has been made at a time when the whole supplementary benefits scheme is under review and when the SBC's chairman has argued that the discretionary elements within supplementary benefits should be limited (Donnison, 1977). 'Is this', social workers ask, 'the thin end of the wedge? Are we to find that we will have to be the main judges of exceptional needs in future?' At the moment social workers' clients are a very small proportion of the people obtaining supplementary benefits. Are they to secure a special passport to ENPs, and if this is the case what effect will that have on the increasing numbers of people knocking on the doors of social services' offices for help with material problems? What will be the consequences for the task if social workers are seen as the people whose help you need if you are to be fairly sure of getting an exceptional payment?

These observations on a new complication in the relationship between the two agencies both suitably ends this discussion and moves us on to the more general policy issues which are the concern of the final chapter.

Chapter 4

Aid, Advice and Advocacy

INTRODUCTION

This chapter brings together the main issues which arise both on social workers' powers to make money payments and on their involvement in assisting clients to obtain help from other sources. It will examine the problems with the way these duties are allocated and put into practice at the moment, and it will attempt to anticipate ways in which developments both within social services departments and within other agencies may affect them in future.

MONEY PAYMENTS AND SOCIAL WORK

Broadly three interlocking problems have been identified about the operation of Section 1 of the Children and Young Persons Act, 1963, Section 12 of the Social Work (Scotland) Act, 1968, and the similar legislation in Northern Ireland. These are:

(1)   the scope for wide variations in the interpretation of the Acts and therefore for inconsistency in their implementation;
(2)   the problem of the relationship between the powers they give to local authorities and those given to the SBC to make exceptional payments;
(3)   the impact of money-giving powers upon social work practice within local authorities.

On the first of these, the scope for variations in the use of the Acts, Chapter 2 cited extensive evidence from national statistics, from our own research and from other studies. It was shown that variations in the use of these powers within authorities are often as great as those, which the national statistics show to be very large, between authorities. While payments are predominantly for three purposes—to meet emergency needs for food, to help with fuel debts and to assist with rent—approaches to these uses vary considerably. Payments are widely made as loans, but there are great variations in willingness to use loans and major problems in securing repayments.

These wide variations may perhaps be justified in terms of (1) the flexibility provided by the discretionary powers involved and (2) the special preventive (or in Scotland 'welfare') requirements for payments. The former argument rests upon a view that individual social workers are close to the 'grass roots' in their own localities and can thus be sensitive to needs and values in the communities which they serve. Exceptional variations may thus be explained by detailed local knowledge, and by a responsiveness to local feeling about justifications for payment. Thus the alleged inconsistencies may be consequences of a desirable local autonomy. Local budgets are set by the local community representatives, the councillors, whose values and assumptions influence the way the local authority's social work staff operate.

Clearly this argument rests upon sentiments widely respected in British local administration today. It is easy to attack it by referring to the evidence that councillors are seldom particularly socially 'representative' of their communities, that local   ections are won and lost on national issues not sensitivity to grass-roots opinion, that local authority social services departments are responsible for areas much larger than single communities, and that social work staff normally penetrate but little into the social systems to which they must relate.

Yet, it may be argued that these facts do not invalidate, indeed in some respects they reinforce, the need to try to decentralise administrative decision making. If that view is taken then, the question to be answered is how far are we prepared to violate territorial justice in the name of local autonomy? The main income maintenance system is provided by a national agency. A small, rather untidy, local system may be tolerable alongside this. But has this new relief 'system' grown too large for its inconsistencies to remain acceptable? Is Jordan right in seeing the emergence of a policy trend which may recreate the Poor Law? This argument deserves particular attention inasmuch as money is being used to meet needs which might equally be met by the national relief system.

The justification for the inconsistencies of Sections 12 and 1 in terms of their functions in promoting welfare and/or preventing children being taken into care is that, of course, these make their use erratic and ensure that there is no clear relationship between needs and payments. Social workers are required, so the Acts suggest, to make very difficult diagnostic judgements in which they make predictions about the probability of family breakdown or other welfare expenditure if money is not forthcoming. Yet do they make decisions in this way? Can they effectively predict? To an extent payments to prevent homelessness can be seen as literally preventing children coming into care, but even in these cases this is only true if social workers are correct in assuming that people saved from eviction would be forced on to the streets and families put into bed and breakfast accommodation would be unable to get anyone else to take them in. Similarly some of the payments of fuel debts may prevent homes becoming unfit places for the care of children, but only if social services departments are in truth the 'last resort'.

The emergency payments for food, however, are very much harder to justify in these terms—particularly as the amounts are generally extremely small, so that very temporary gaps in the family budgets are being plugged. In a cumulative sense a family unable to make ends meet may in due course 'break down'. But in this case the income maintenance problems are unlikely to be solved by isolated payments and local authorities are certainly not willing to contemplate regular weekly supplements to poor families.

However, it seems most improbable that the very inconsistent variations in the money payments can be explained by variations in vulnerability to family breakdown. At a high level of generality it is entirely appropriate that some of the authorities with very large numbers of family problems on their hands are also high users of the powers to make cash payments. Yet, as was suggested, the statistical evidence for this tendency in England and Wales largely derives from the way in which the London, and particularly the inner London, authorities stand out on all the indices of social services needs and expenditure. At a lower level this argument cannot explain some of the striking variations between adjacent authorities, or within authorities.

This issue of inconsistency should not only be raised in terms of territorial injustice. Social workers' powers to make payments are totally discretionary; clients have no 'rights' to help. Concern with this issue led Michael Adler to suggest that there should be a formal 'framework' for the making of decisions about financial assistance. He proposed the following four regulations (1974, p.41):

1. Each local authority should formulate rules, regulations and guidelines relating to the circumstances in which people may be assisted financially, the manner in which they may be assisted, e.g. whether by a loan or by a grant, and the maximum extent of assistance, all such rules, regulations and guidelines to be made public.

2. Each local authority should specify the limits to the powers of social workers at various levels of seniority to make decisions relating to financial assistance, this too to be made public.
3. All requests for financial assistance should be answered in writing and all decisions should be made in terms of the administrative rules, regulations and guidelines laid down by the local authority.
4. Dissatisfied clients should have the right to a second opinion and/or the opportunity to appeal to an independent tribunal which could likewise decide their case in relation to the rules, regulations and guidelines adopted by the local authority concerned.

Adler, very rightly, draws our attention to the lack of a framework of rules to govern policies in this area. Social workers regularly criticise SBC staff for arbitrary decision making, talk of 'welfare *rights*', and assist clients to appeal against supplementary benefits decisions. It is important to remind them that clients have no means of challenging their own decisions about cash payments. But is it appropriate to formalise Section 1 and Section 12 decision making in this way? To do so seems to involve recognition that they form a viable part of the social security system. If one believes that money payments should be kept at a minimum such an action would surely push the system in the wrong direction.

Both Section 1 and Section 12 are worded, as has been shown, so that their 'exceptional' and 'preventative' use is stressed. This is particularly true of Section 1. Would a dissatisfied client appeal against a refusal of help on the grounds that he was thereby forced to abandon his child? Formalisation, here, would encourage a form of blackmail ('I will leave my child in your office if you don't help me') which both social workers and SBC officials experience from time to time. Surely, Adler's propositions could not be adopted without some redrafting of the statutes to remove the emphasis upon the use of money for 'casework' ends. In his article he rightly reminds us, as have writers like Handler and Jordan who emphasise the 'social control' aspect of the giving of money, that the decision making on financial assistance is not really a skilled and subtle exercise of professional discretion; his solution to the problem that this raises makes only too apparent the ways in which Sections 1 and 12 hang awkwardly between 'preventative' social work and supplementary income maintenance.

The second problem identified at the beginning of this chapter was the relationship between these grant-giving powers and SBC powers to meet exceptional needs. As suggested above, the maintenance of a consistent relationship between these two sources of support for poor families is important if the argument for local autonomy is to be sustained. While a case may be made for locally inspired variations in payments of some special kind, it is very difficult to justify variations in the extent to which local agencies take over financial burdens from a national agency which is expected to be 'even-handed' throughout the country. Here, incidentally, lies another difficulty about Adler's proposals. He suggests a need for local consistency in a context of legitimate variations between authorities. The formalisation of the system in this way would further enhance the difficulties of liaison between the SBC and individual local authorities.

The data reported in this book do not *prove* that there are local variations in the extent to which clients can get help from social services instead of supplementary benefits. To do this would have required a very elaborate (indeed probably impossible) project surveying the total extent to which needs are met by either agency. However, it seems very probable that such variations occur on account of (1) the wide variations in the extent to which social services departments make money payments, (2) the fact that many cash recipients are on supplementary benefits, whilst at the same time the proportions of such families on supplementary benefits vary from authority to authority, (3) that a high proportion of payments by social services departments are for needs which the SBC can meet and (4) that social workers vary markedly in their willingness to seek SBC help for their clients.

Clients are likely to become aware that there are inconsistencies and a lack of clear boundary drawn between the responsibilities of the agencies. Occasionally they may exploit the lack of clarity. In other cases they may be puzzled by 'deals' between the departments in which their exceptional needs are partly met by each agency. In many cases they may feel able to go on to social services for help in situations in which supplementary benefits have been refused. Often they may see no logic in a refusal in circumstances in which, on other occasions, they have received help, but they will be appeased by the fact that they can get aid from an alternative source. The way in which, as the fuel boards' 'code of practice' showed, other agencies regard the SBC and social services as alternative sources of help, and the way in which the media frequently confuse social services and social security, encourage a view that the two kinds of agencies have broadly overlapping functions.

There has been an extensive debate about this uneasy boundary. The primary sources of criticism of the role played by the SBC in relation to this boundary are Emmett and Lister's *Under the Safety Net* and Ruth Lister's 'open letter' to David Donnison in *Social Work Today*. *Assistance in Cash,* a pamphlet produced jointly by the SBC and the local authority associations, is an attempt to clarify the position, but the main sources of the SBC viewpoint are Professor Donnison's comments on Emmett and Lister's pamphlet in *SBC Notes and News,* together with his reply in *Social Work Today* to Ruth Lister's 'open letter'.

The attack on the SBC rests primarily upon an argument that the many exceptional needs, and in particular those of SBC claimants, being met by social services departments should be met by the SBC. The response to this is that the SBC must draw the line somewhere. It is very clearly stressed that supplementary benefits will not normally be available to families where the breadwinner is in full-time work. In other situations the position is, according to *Assistance in Cash,* as follows (para. 16):

> They [exceptional needs] may also arise where, although the claimant is within the field of supplementary benefit, the local officer of the Commission decides that an exceptional needs payment could not be justified within the Commission's policy. Such a decision is made without regard to the fact that the social services departments may have power to assist, but if the social services departments then wish to consider providing assistance under their own power (perhaps after consultation with the Commission's officers) it is open to them to do so.

This quotation stresses that the SBC must draw some lines beyond which payments will not be made. After that, if a local authority still chooses to pay that is its affair.

A concern with 'welfare rights' necessarily involves not merely a demand that SBC fulfils its statutory obligations but also a requirement that it recognises in a clear and coherent way the limits of its responsibilities. Earlier in this chapter it was suggested that one of the major problems with Sections 1 and 12 is the extent to which their use seems to violate considerations of territorial justice. The SBC has a territorial justice problem too. In its *Annual Report 1976* the Commission acknowledges that 'the highest local office ratio of ENPs to workload can be as much as ten or eleven times

that of the office with the lowest ratio' (p. 111). The review of the
SBC scheme being undertaken, at the time of writing, is concerned,
amongst other things, to achieve greater consistency within the
system. Social workers who are concerned about the SBC's
reluctance to make some kinds of payments should regard this with
sympathy, inasmuch as it involves an attempt to achieve
consistency. In its *Annual Report 1976* the SBC argues (p. 192):

> Our relationships with Social Services Departments were beset in
> the past by a feeling not uncommon amongst social workers that
> financial needs were to be met primarily, it not exclusively, by
> the Commission, and the Social Services Departments should be
> concerned only with social needs. This is a simplification which
> leads to the conclusion that there is no financial problem which it
> is not for the Commission to solve and ignores the legislative
> limits to our functions. In exercising our discretion we must
> recognise these limitations just as much as the requirement 'to
> promote the welfare' of the people with whom we deal. We
> must also have an eye for the political constraints on any social
> assistance scheme. Constantly extending our discretionary
> provision may result in so alienating those whom we cannot or
> do not help that the whole supplementary benefits scheme falls
> into disrepute.

It is important, when reading this, to bear in mind the pressure
upon the SBC to become involved in an increasingly complex way
with the solution of fuel cost problems (this is explored further in
the Appendix). It is also significant that the SBC faces other
awkward boundary problems with local government, with some
authorities ever eager to pass specific costs on to central
government by refusing benefits to supplementary benefits
recipients. In the past some rent rebate schemes were designed to
achieve this objective. More recently some social services
departments have tried to get the SBC to meet home help charges,
and some education departments have sought to shift some of their
'discretionary' obligations to help with school uniform costs on to
the SBC.

None the less, the SBC's *Annual Report 1976* suggests a view of
the social worker's dilemma, which, as the evidence reported in this
book shows, is a gross oversimplification (loc. cit.): 'Similarly, the
idea that financial needs are irrelevant to "real" social work
problems is both an over narrow view of the functions of Social
Services Departments and of social workers and implies a rigid

categorisation of types of problems which rarely occurs in reality.' There is a large gap, unrecognised in that statement, between regarding financial needs as not 'irrelevant' to 'social work problems', and regarding it as appropriate that social workers should have the powers to meet those needs!

The assumption implicit in *Assistance in Cash* that a clear and logical boundary is, and can be, drawn around the responsibilities of the SBC has, so far, been left unquestioned in this discussion. The research findings suggest that the 'boundary' is certainly not very skilfully drawn in practice. SBC refusals to make emergency payments because local offices will not fit claimants into an appointments system, and to meet fuel bills because others have been met in the past, are not very good examples of boundary drawing. Ruth Lister and Tony Emmett, writing as members of the 'poverty lobby', refrain from canvassing very fully one option open to deal with this boundary problem, presumably for fear of the hardship it might pose for claimants: that the social services departments should be very much less willing to meet needs which the SBC refuses to meet. While this might intensify conflict between social services departments and SBC local offices it would, logically, be an effective approach to many of the boundary issues since, relative to the SBC, the social services departments play such a minor role in meeting needs. Moreover, such a development might well produce the result Lister and Emmett desire since it seems likely to be easier for local SBC staff to say 'no' when they know they are not the last source of help. It might be much less easy to do so if, once again, it was clear that the ultimate responsibility was in their hands.

To what extent, it may be asked, does the argument developed here suggest that Section 1 and Section 12 should be abolished? Or does it merely imply that their use should, as the British Association of Social Workers has suggested, be radically curtailed? How seriously are we to take the view, clearly held by many social workers in the early sixties, that without some money-giving powers social workers are either, at worst, severely limited in the constructive work they can do to keep children out of care (and thus, of course, incur enormous public expense, let alone cause unquantifiable private harm) or at best dependent upon uncertain charitable help for preventive work. Certainly this view must be respected. The challenge to those who take it is to try to work out a way of confining the use of the money-giving powers. Is it possible to define the 'exceptional' preventive use of money so that it cannot be subject to the continual widening which has been experienced since 1963? Tony Emmett pointed out the crucial difficulty when he argued, at a seminar on this issue, that it is normal for people to try to qualify for cash assistance and, arguably, a failure to do so may be an indication of social pathology. Therefore, where it is known that an agency has wide discretionary powers to provide cash there will be a demand for the provision of financial assistance, and the more assistance is given, the more will be demanded by potential claimants.

The BASW policy statement on this issue contains two propositions relevant here: 'Cash should normally be paid only to clients not eligible under the 1966 Ministry of Social Security Act'; and 'Cash help should be given in the context of the existing worker/client contact with a view to providing time for work with the underlying causes of the social problems being experienced. Lack of adequate means should not normally justify cash aid from social workers except in exceptional circumstances.' The first of the propositions is carefully qualified by reference to exceptional situations where the 'client is too frail—emotionally or physically', and the second is hedged around with words like 'normally' and 'exceptionally'. How far can a strong stand be taken on the present legislation, and how far is the pressure towards a looser interpretation bound to continue?

There are significant parallels here with the work being done by the Supplementary Benefits Commission to try to find ways of limiting its own powers to make exceptional payments. The central difficulty is that exceptional situations are by definition the unexpected and unanticipated, and are thus not readily susceptible to tight definition in such a way that a large number of more common situations are excluded. Both the SBC and social services departments have to acknowledge that, while they can emphasise over and over again that fuel debts, or rents, for example, should be met out of other income, and should not be regarded as exceptional, nevertheless someone about to lose his or her fuel supply or be evicted is in a crisis situation, in which family members may be harmed. Moreover, such a crisis is always likely to be seen as more deserving of 'exceptional' use of some supply of cash for special situations than someone seeking money for some more unusual need. To take an example from the pilot survey to our Section 1 study, is the use of money to enable a hard-pressed mother to go to art classes a 'better' use of Section 1 than a payment of a fuel debt? It is certainly an 'exceptional', 'constructive' and 'preventive' use of money, yet it is hard for a social worker or a local authority to justify such a choice between needs. It is this argument that leads us to be uneasy about solutions to this problem which fall short of the repeal of social services' money-giving powers. However, we too must be realistic, since it is such compromise solutions which are most probable. One such approach involves attempting to confine payments to families where the prevention of the provision of care is quite explicitly central to the decision. Our doubts about this rest upon diagnostic difficulty outlined above. It provides one approach to a much tougher line by social services departments. It will not, however, altogether eliminate the niggling 'boundary' problem we have described.

This concern with the boundary between the supplementary benefits scheme and income maintenance from social services departments assumes a significance out of proportion either to the present extent of the overlap or the present scale of the use of Sections 1 and 12 because SBC policies are changing and are likely to change further. Many social services staff fear that, when the chairman of the SBC stresses that his organisation's use of its discretionary powers has got out of hand—leading to inequitable decision making, distortion of the meaning of 'exceptional' and high administrative costs (Donnison, 1977)—a series of simplifications will be introduced into the supplementary benefits' scheme which leave social services departments to deal with a wide range of 'exceptional' income-maintenance problems.

At the time of writing a team of civil servants reviewing the supplementary benefits scheme has suggested a series of simplifications (see *Social Assistance,* DHSS, 1978), some of which will limit local office discretion. While they do not involve the delegation of money-giving powers to social services departments, some social workers believe that the proposals may have this effect. They fear that once the SBC starts to stand firm on a framework of more rigid rules, once it stresses that 'exceptional' means what it says, then the pressure for help under Sections 1 and 12 will automatically increase. This is particularly likely if the revision of the supplementary benefits scheme is not accompanied by any substantial increase in the amount of money provided by the basic scale rates.

One current development which is reinforcing social workers' fears on this issue is the arrangement, discussed in Chapter 3, that, in some circumstances, ENPs may be granted on their recommendations alone. To what extent, they ask, is this relatively minor change in SBC internal working rules a foretaste of more extensive changes to come?

The final problem about social workers' financial powers which we must discuss is their impact upon social work practice. In Chapter 1, Jordan's view that the linking together of social work with income maintenance is re-creating the Poor Law was briefly quoted. Jordan is strongly committed to social casework. He argues (1974, p.102):

> Casework is an approach to a helping relationship which is based on compassion for people in trouble, sorrow, need, sickness and various other adversities. Properly applied casework is a necessary condition for the humane and decent provision of certain services for people in various kinds of emotional distress, in crisis, suffering bereavement, trauma or despair.

He rejects the radical attack on social casework *per se* as 'an instrument of class oppression', arguing that social work's critics have been misled by the 'evidence from social services departments which have been increasingly used for tasks of income maintenance, which have perverted the original purpose of social work training'. It is his view (ibid., p.107) that

> casework can, and does, flourish in the service of clients' needs both as a public provision and as a private enterprise, virtually unrelated to the economic demands of the productive system, provided that certain conditions are realised ... one important set of conditions is connected with the purposes of those who employ caseworkers, and ... one particular purpose (public assistance) is particularly fatal to good casework as it is generally understood.

In Chapter 2 it was shown that many social workers share Jordan's concern about the impact of income maintenance duties upon their work. They argue that social work objectives become confused and that clients find it difficult to distinguish between their responsibilities and the duties of SBC staff. While some social workers cheerfully accept a situation in which they may use their money-giving powers to bargain with clients, very many feel profoundly uneasy about the extent to which they possess this kind of power. The issue here involves both considerations about social work practice and about social work ethics, although for many social workers these two are always closely inter-related.

Many social workers acknowledge that Jordan has issued an important warning about the dangers inherent in the powers given under Sections 1 and 12. But to what extent is he dealing with a danger which lies in the future rather than with a problem which already exists? And to what extent does he damage his own argument by overstatement? It is important to remember that Handler, whose evidence Jordan uses, is an American whose primary concern in writing of the 'coercive social worker' was to draw attention, by the use of British examples, to a problem of fundamental importance, as Keith-Lucas has shown, for public social work in his own country. The scale of money payments within British social work is comparatively slight. The most important reason for giving attention to these arguments is, as suggested above, the possibility that financial responsibilities will be delegated to social workers on a much greater scale in the future.

Money payments by social workers are quite rare. In England and Wales no more than 5 million pounds a year is spent under Section 1 of the Children and Young Persons Act, 1963. At the same time the SBC paid out, in 1976, £1,537 million including £24 million on exceptional needs payments. Most payments to individuals, as we have seen, are very small. They are essentially occasional payments for special purposes. It may be argued that to call this 'income maintenance' is to mislead, and to get the social control problem out of proportion. In the quotation from *Claimant or Client?* on p. 45 Olive Stevenson drew a distinction between 'basic allowances' and 'extras' and suggested that this distinction together with honesty about the bargains involved can impose important limitations upon the extent of the problem.

We may suggest, then, that considerations of scale have an important influence upon the degree to which Jordan's warning must be taken seriously. There is scope for disagreement, however, about the level at which occasional 'extras' begin to become a significant contribution to income maintenance.

But there is another, perhaps more important way in which Jordan's argument misleads us. Olive Stevenson dealt with this in her paper to the Cropwood Conference on 'Social services as controllers'. She argued that there are many other ways, more important that the administration of money payments for British social services, in which social workers find themselves in social control roles. The protection of the weak and vunerable inevitably involves controlling some people's behaviour, but above all 'any meaningful encounter between human beings involves power relations in which one seeks to influence another' and the notion of liberty to which practice must relate 'is at all times and in all places conditional upon a given social order'. Indeed we will suggest below that, in relationships with clients, aid and advocacy may also be a service given in return for compliance and conformity. Aspects of social control permeate social worker/client relationships of all kinds; the money-giving issue should not be singled out as special in this respect.

The local authority social worker is (1) in a relationship in which —inasmuch as his help, advice, friendship or support is needed— there is an inherent 'power' element, (2) likely to be in a situation, at least in working with a family, in which his power in the last resort to remove children from the care of their parents is not absent from some of his clients' minds and (3) able to make money payments. The last of these sources of power is likely to be the least. It must be remembered that Section 1 money-giving powers exist to help prevent reception of children into care. In this respect any social worker who is properly mindful of the statutory limitations upon his money-granting power is possessed of two alternative means of 'social control'—the 'stick' of removal of children from the family, and the 'carrot' of money payments. The latter may be more insidious than the former, but without it the power relationship would be little different.

This section has dealt with three kinds of arguments against Sections 1 and 12. It has suggested that the first two are, in the present situation, the most important, while the third draws our attention to some of the longer-run dangers in a developing and changing pattern of income maintenance.

Jordan paints a picture of social casework in which he makes light of the other sources of social worker power. It is quite clear from his book that his ideal for a public social work service is one in which the present tendency for social work to be primarily with the poor and deprived is eliminated through radical improvements in the other services of the 'welfare state'. This 'utopian' vision leads him to give insufficient attention to the extent to which social workers, even when they are not concerned with determining eligibility for money payments, are involved with helping poor people to solve income-maintenance and related material-need problems. This advice and advocacy work raises a number of problems about the relationship between it and other forms of social work, and also therefore a number of problems about power and social control, which are deserving of attention in their own right.

ADVICE AND ADVOCACY IN SOCIAL WORK

In the area terms studied, social workers became involved in a variety of ways in advising clients who were having difficulties in getting help from other agencies. They also, to varying degrees, sought to contact agencies on their clients' behalf. Relatively few social workers saw such work as central, though many acknowledged that they spent considerable amounts of time on such tasks. Furthermore, very few saw themselves as 'welfare rights' advocates in any very 'militant' sense. Indeed, few had accompanied clients to appeal tribunals. While social workers acknowledged that sometimes their main role in these matters was simply to encourage clients to 'stand up for themselves', in very many situations they argued that their involvement required efforts to present clients' cases to the other agencies. Hence social workers made a variety of remarks of which the following are typical:

> I think we have a better relationship with these agencies than the client does. I think we can usually get a better deal ...

> all you do is telephone them and try and sort out and put the client's problem in a different way, probably articulate them better, and quite often it is sorted out. It seems to me a bit silly that it couldn't have been sorted out before you had to intervene, but if there was more understanding of the problem and people were willing to give a little bit more time and to help people to articulate then this could be sorted out at the initial department without having to come to us and then go back to them as it always does.

> I think your role is that of advocate very often ... you are giving the client an opportunity, when he's not made angry or upset, to state clearly what it is he's after; so that you have information which you can hopefully give in a coherent manner to the person at the other end ... You're doing advocacy and interpretation and also informing the client what his rights are, or ways of getting things that maybe he didn't know about. For instance, a lot of folk just walk into DHSS offices and say 'I want to make a claim for supplementary benefits', and they say 'Go away'.

> Well, repairs to houses, especially elderly people. When they ask the rent man it goes in such a roundabout way sometimes repair requests take weeks. If we get on to the telephone and stress to the housing department this is an elderly person and ask for priority ...

Only the third of these quotations involves the exposition of a comparatively coherent 'welfare rights' approach. The others were just saying 'We get attention when the client doesn't'. Many social workers stressed that it should not be necessary if only the system were simpler and the 'bureaucratic' barriers easier to cross.

A few social workers were very reluctant to become involved in activity of this kind. Some of the hospital social workers were perhaps most outspoken in this respect. One argued:

> It's not the task of the social worker to be an expert on social security. If there's a social security problem I'll refer it to ... [the local office] and say 'that's your problem but I will help you by giving you the facts as I see them'.

One field social worker went so far as to see a conflict between welfare advice work and other aspects of his task:

> When you start to be seen as the welfare man ... your credibility in terms of help with relationships ... the expertise you bring to situations can be reduced and diluted.

While only a few of the social workers studied would have disagreed strongly with these standpoints, many clearly saw this 'welfare' work as something which arose, for better or for worse, out of casework relationships, and had to be tackled, but not as work that was positively welcomed.

There are a number of reasons why people come to social services departments with problems about relations with the various agencies providing welfare benefits. In some of the more stressful areas, notably in the inner cities, it would be a peculiarly insensitive social worker who did not frequently detect material problems of fundamental significance for his client's social functioning. Moreover, everywhere clients face problems of this kind alongside other problems. Hence, even if social workers were generally regarded as in no way concerned with such issues they could not totally escape them. However, people bring material problems to social services departments because they are confused about 'who does what' in the welfare state, and because these departments do give help in kind, and sometimes even in cash. Some of these people could be turned away by 'tough' receptionists; indeed, as Anthony Hall has shown, some are. Social services departments, and therefore social workers, are faced by difficult dilemmas about being 'tough', about arguing that they are not the agency to help with these problems. Having helped with some problems of this kind, particularly if they have given money in some circumstances, they are faced by grave difficulties about turning others away. A reputation as a helping agency, once acquired, may lead to a mushrooming growth of demands for help.

The research did not attempt to quantify the amounts of social work time given to aid, advice and advocacy. It is not possible to say whether the departments which made money payments, or were more ready to engage in negotiations with the DHSS, experienced greater pressure from clients for help of this kind. In particular this study does not answer the important question, which needs to be asked, about the extent to which this work is growing. What it does show is that social workers generally seemed to accept work of this kind, whilst not in many cases having a very clear conception of the place of such activity within social work. It was widely seen as a 'necessary evil' of work in a local authority department. Except perhaps to some extent in the rare cases where duty work was seen as a specialism, it was not regarded as a specialised aspect of social work, but rather as something with which everyone had to cope. The extent to which social workers became involved, and the way in which they did so, depended very much upon individual ideologies, upon personal views about the place of social work in the welfare state. Just as we know that clients seeking monetary help from social services departments may have very different success, from authority to authority, area to area and social worker to social worker, so much the same can probably be said about the extent to which they get other kinds of help with social security or housing problems. Nevertheless, it was suggested that clients' expectations of help of either kind appears to grow and grow. While many social workers protest that such work is 'not efficient use of time', they feel they cannot escape it because they are at the end of the line for needy people:

> It really does stop here—you feel that everything is dropping into the bottom of the barrel and it can't get back out again. You can't refer [clients] anywhere else after they've been here; they've been round the rest first.

The picture of advice and advocacy work presented by a high proportion of the social workers interviewed is one which throws doubts upon the widespread description of this as 'welfare rights' work. Rarely were social workers engaged in fighting for rights in any strong sense; rather they were giving advice and intervening with other agencies in situations in which they felt clients faced difficulties in presenting their own caes. When they dealt with SBC staff or with officials from housing departments or fuel boards they generally expected to adopt a conciliatory stance and to negotiate, not to assert 'rights'. For most of them, too, a failure to gain anything for a client was the end of the process. Few social workers had been involved in helping clients take supplementary benefits cases to appeal, and there was no evidence in these areas, at the time of the studies, of social workers engaging in more activist 'lobbying' tactics. In this sense some of the discussions of social workers' involvement with welfare rights campaigns in the press convey an impression of militancy to other agencies which do not seem to be borne out by day-to-day practice.

Indeed the picture painted here suggests an alternative danger. This is that social workers may be discredited in the eyes of some of their clients by the extent of their 'co-optation'. They may be seen as only taking up the 'good' cases with the SBC, letting the definition of good cases be determined by the latter agency. In this sense advice and advocacy may draw social workers as readily into the 'social security system' as does direct responsibility for money payments. The giving of help in negotiating with or appealing against another agency, or the refusal of that help, within a social work relationship, involve elements of social control in their own right. They may not be as obvious as those entailed in giving or refusing money payments, but they too convey messages to the client about the acceptability of his behaviour and the extent to which he is regarded as a 'deserving case'. It is not our purpose here to advocate that the social worker's stance should necessarily be 'my client, right or wrong', but merely to set this discussion of advice and advocacy in the context of the earlier examination of the place of social control in this part of the social work task. The social worker engaged in advocacy must make his own choice of the right position between the Scylla of a total and negative 'war' against the SBC which may be very unrewarding to those he is trying to help, and the Charybdis of a role in which he is regularly engaged in putting the SBC's point of view to his clients.

Relatively few of a sample of social work students, who were asked at the end of their course about their attitudes to various tasks they might have to do once back in practice, said they liked working on clients' financial problems. Nearly all regarded it as probable that they would have to do such work. Replies to a further questionnaire sent to these students, about nine months after they had left their course, confirmed that they were right.

Almost all had encountered work of this kind. Is this one of the facts of life about local authority social work? Should social work students be taught that this is the reality which they must face? Ought they accordingly to be equipped to deal with such work as effectively as possible? Or can the amount of such work coming to social workers be reduced to leave them free for other aspects of social casework? Is it bound to grow, or are there conditions in which it could decline to unimportance?

The answers to these questions depend upon four things: the extent to which weaknesses in other agencies and their policies throw up, and must continue to throw up, problems for social workers' clients; the extent to which alternative sources of advice and advocacy can shift the burden of such work away from social services departments; the degree to which social workers and their departments operate policies and practices which attract clients who ask for, or need, help in their dealings with social security offices and with their creditors; and the readiness of social services departments to employ staff who may take over such work from social workers. Let us look at each of these in turn.

At a simple level, the problems for clients arising from the 'weaknesses of other agencies' may be described as unmet needs. Many of the problems brought to social workers may be said to derive from 'gaps' in the pattern of welfare provision. However, where other agencies have not met, and *cannot* meet, particular needs, there may be little that social workers can do. Accordingly the situations which create the most work for social workers are those in which other organisations appear to have the duty, capacity or power to help but have not done so. A great deal of advice and advocacy work is required because of the complexity of the welfare system and the lack of clarity about 'rights'. Clients require help in finding their way through the tangle of inter-related and overlapping social security benefit provisions. They need advice on how to obtain many of the more obscure means-tested benefits. They need advocates to argue about their needs for discretionary benefits. The incremental character of legislative innovation is steadily making the mixture of benefits more complex. Recent additions to the social security system which cause particular confusion are earnings-related contributory benefits, family income supplement, new benefits for the disabled such as attendance allowance and mobility allowance and a variety of *ad hoc* additions to means-tested benefits such as electricity bill discounts and reliefs from health service and local government charges.

In Chapter 3 examples were quoted from interviews with social workers of situations in which clients needed help because of the treatment they received at the hands of officials. Social workers argued that they sometimes needed to intervene simply to ensure that clients' cases were heard properly. At one level such problems may be attributed to organisational weaknesses in other agencies—the lack of adequate information about benefits, poor reception facilities, insufficient staff training and a lack of effective measures to prevent rude and unhelpful behaviour by front-line staff. Yet many of these weaknesses are closely associated with the complexity of the rules about entitlement to benefits. Junior staff dealing with the public may be themselves uncertain about what they have to offer. They may also find difficulty in relating clients' circumstances to their rules. Their negative behaviour may be a consequence of irritation and frustration with difficulties in administering the benefits for which they are responsible.

Social workers sometimes argue that much of the welfare rights work they have to do would not arise if other organisations functioned satisfactorily. Of course, this is often true. Many problems would not be brought to them if, for example, receptionists at social security offices or housing departments always did their jobs properly. But they should not underestimate the difficulties faced by staff in other departments. In this respect any simplification of social security which can be achieved may significantly reduce pressures upon social workers. Such releif may even be brought about by reforms which make 'rights' more explicit without necessarily making any further help available. However, if one argues that the best way to reduce welfare rights work is to ensure that other agencies function better, it is important to bear in mind the extent to which the effective working of the system may actually depend upon advocacy. It is unrealistic to expect that an agency dispensing discretionary benefits will readily seek out those who may need its help. Many of the rules governing the provisions of the welfare state are inherently ambiguous. The contesting of individual cases is often necessary to establish precedents and working rules. It is unrealistic to expect that reforms will eliminate situations in which clients who have difficulty in arguing their own cases need the help of advocates. It is equally unrealistic to expect that the departments dispensing benefits will provide staff willing and able to argue cases against their own organisations. Welfare law, however well codified it may become, needs to be developed and enforced through argument about cases, just like any other part of our system of law.

This leads us to the second determinant of the degree to which social workers need to be involved in advice and advocacy work: the extent to which such work is done by other organisations. One alternative way of looking at this work is to regard it as legal, or quasi-legal, work. The 'welfare rights' approach to this work emphasises this aspect, against those who prefer to see the determination of needs to welfare benefits, at the margin, as an essentially discretionary activity in which provisions are related to individual circumstances. Some opponents of the welfare rights approach portray their alternative as an exercise in 'social work'. Their view is that decision making should be governed by a very close knowledge of individual circumstances in which notions of 'rights' are misleading and undermine precision in the making of decisions. One of the difficulties facing social workers who engage in *rights* work is that others, their 'antagonists' and sometimes their 'employers', expect them to see issues in this alternative way. They expect them to assist with the making of discretionary decisions and not to fight them. It is the clash between these two alternative conceptions which lies at the core of the uncertainty and controversy described earlier as arising from the SBC's suggestion to its staff that exceptional needs payments may be made on social workers' recommendations.

Given this uncertainty about the most appropriate role for the social worker, together with all his other different responsibilities, it seems logical to argue that the best source of aid and advocacy for claimants is an independent advice centre backed up by legal expertise. Social services departments, as agencies with benefit-giving responsibilities of their own, a need to acknowledge, at a national level, an underlying working relationship with the DHSS, and a dependence upon public funds, are not the very best organisations to adopt an adversary stance towards other public bodies. As the Wolfenden Committee argue: 'Where the performance of statutory agencies is what is at issue the consumer will need the support of an independent organisation' (1978, p. 60).

Hence one important response to the growing need for welfare rights advice is to urge, not that social services departments should get better at this work, but that efforts should be made to stimulate the growth of separate advice service. There are several options: the development of more voluntary agencies, with the support of grants from public bodies; the further growth of welfare rights services attached to Citizens' Advice Bureaux; the development of such advice services under local government control but not attached to specific departments; or even the funding of welfare rights staff attached to health clinics. Yet all these are ideal solutions, heavily dependent upon large fresh injections of public money, while social services departments are very much involved in welfare rights work already. Only in a few, largely urban areas, do there already exist strong alternative agencies to which social workers can refer clients in need of this kind of help.

It was suggested that the extent of advice and advocacy work for social workers is considerably influenced by the extent to which people with welfare rights problems are drawn to seek help from this source. Goldberg and her colleagues, reporting on their study of social services 'intake' in Southampton, show that the teams whose work they monitored faced twice as many clients presenting financial and material difficulties in 1975 as they did in 1973. They comment (1977, p. 263):

> This large increase was also noted in a study of social services consumers in the same city and probably reflects the consequences of rising unemployment and inflation. The comments of the consumers also suggested that the social services department is increasingly used as an information and advice centre and as a referral agency, particularly in relation to financial difficulties.

While we must beware of generalising from one particular study, in which the monitoring of referrals made social workers particularly self-conscious about their own practices in accepting or rejecting various kinds of work, there seems no reason to suggest that the Southampton experience will have been very different from that in other parts of the country.

It is, of course, difficult to disentangle the effects of 'rising unemployment and inflation', and changing social security policies and practices, from the factors that lead consumers to see social services as sources of information and advice. It is also difficult to determine how much this perception of social services departments as advice agencies is influenced by their own policies. However, it seems likely that if social workers are increasingly aware of the 'welfare rights' dimension in their work, and are making increasing efforts to solve clients' material problems, this will alter the way what they have to offer is perceived both by existing clients and by others who learn about their 'successes' in work of this kind. Social workers who, rightly in our view, perceive that it is necessary to sort out pressing material problems alongside their other work with clients, have to face the fact that their very success in dealing with 'presenting problems' increases their own 'bombardment' with such problems.

This developing image of social services departments as agencies which may be approached by clients with material problems is further enhanced by the powers they possess to give direct help. In this respect numbers of money payments made may be but the tip of a large iceberg. For every client receiving a Section 1 payment, there may be a host of others who approach the department in hope of such payments but secure advice or advocacy instead. Clients, even if they are not actually confused about the distinction between social services and social security, come to recognise that there are a number of different ways social workers may help them with material-needs problems. We have already shown that other agencies collude with this situation by encouraging debtors to approach social services. Hence the growth of money payments and the growth of aid and advocacy proceed in step, each stimulating the other.

In our view this is a development which is very hard to resist. It can be stemmed, *now,* only by radical changes in the social security system or by the large-scale growth of other advice and advocacy agencies. It certainly cannot be stemmed by unilateral action by social services departments, unless social workers are to adopt a peculiarly insensitive approach to their clients' material problems, which many social workers would regard as unjustifiable. The material problems are there. So long as social workers try to do something about them they will be perceived as people who help with problems of that kind, and the 'bombardment' will continue. Of course one consideration which may deter departments from responding effectively to this kind of pressure is the fear that such responses will themselves escalate the growth of such work. They hope that if the extent to which they provide this sort of help remains patchy and inadequate, other things will change, other agencies will arise, and the problem will gradually go away. In discussing how best to organise for this work we are suggesting not merely that such work will not readily go away, but also that advice and advocacy is important. In this we agree with Wootton and Sinfield. We differ from them in a reluctance to argue or imply that it is necessarily more important than other aspects of the social work task. We believe that it can, and perhaps should, be tackled separately from, but alongside, other social work activities.

While social workers do often have to help their long-term clients to solve material problems, a considerable proportion of this work arises at the 'intake' stage. New clients and, increasingly, clients who have been seen before but who are not getting regular social work help, seek aid with these problems from staff concerned with the reception of new work. Goldberg and her colleagues showed how, in the Southampton teams, 17 per cent of the problems at 'first referral' were 'financial or material', and 11 per cent were concerned with 'housing or accommodation'. A further 30 per cent of referrals were classified as involving as the main problem 'physical disability, illness or ageing', and their discussion of these suggests that many involved material needs. They present a very interesting table (Goldberg *et al.,* p. 270) which shows that a high proportion of the cases in which the presenting problems were material needs were closed very quickly. After one day 75 per cent of all cases remained open, but only 52 per cent of the 'financial/material' group. After one week the respective percentages were 53 and 30 per cent; after one month they were 36 and 15 per cent.

One aspect of the Southampton research was the completion of a case record that was likely to have made social workers conscious of the need to 'close' cases quickly where they felt that they were limited in the effective work they could do. This may have heightened the contrast between material problem referrals and others. On the other hand a sophisticated review system might have been expected to make them conscious of the extent to which material 'presenting problems' were masking deeper problems of other kinds. On balance, the Southampton evidence does seem very suggestive of the extent to which work on material problems is distinguishable 'short-term' work. Social services staff in Southampton may encounter very many more referrals of this kind than their rural colleagues. We should not presume that the proportion of such work will be as high everywhere else. But equally it seems plausible to suggest that there may be areas—inner London, Glasgow, Liverpool, for example—where it is very much higher. In all the areas where 'intake' work on material problems reaches a significant proportion is it not worthwhile considering whether such work justifies a specialised response?

The case for specialised welfare rights work does not rest upon the evidence on the volume of referrals alone. Welfare rights advice is needed from time to time in the course of a great deal of other social work, some of it long-term, and much of it not classifiable as solely work on material problems. However, we must distinguish between work on which the welfare rights help will be the central social services input from that in which it will be more peripheral. In the former case direct referral to a specialist may be appropriate;

in the latter a specialist may need to be seen primarily as a resource to his colleagues.

It has been established that advice and advocacy work takes up a considerable, and probably increasing, proportion of social workers' time. Its maximum impact is upon 'duty' and short-term work. It is often unpopular with social workers, and it requires an extensive and growing body of specialised knowledge. Would it not be appropriate, therefore, for many field teams in the social services to include within their ranks a welfare rights specialist? Such a person could be a trained social worker with a special interest in this work. But it might be equally appropriate to employ for such a post someone with an extensive knowledge of welfare benefits and welfare law who was not also a qualified social worker. The argument for the latter kind of person is, of course, strengthened by the scarcity of trained social workers and by the problems entailed in including comprehensive welfare rights training within social work courses.

The whole drift of the argument over the last few pages has been to suggest the case for such a worker. What is the case against? First of all, we are far from clear about the true volume of work of this kind. It depends significantly upon the area served. It has also been suggested that it is likely to be affected by the extent to which material need referrals are encouraged. It is clear from the Southampton figures that 17 per cent of the referrals does not necessarily imply 17 per cent of the work. Such cases were seldom held long, though they may have been very time-consuming during the period they were held. It is very hard to even guess how many teams there are where work of this kind would justify a full-time appointment. On the other hand there are a variety of other duties with which it may be combined, not least the considerable volume of work entailed in organising social service provisions—day care, domestic help, telephones, aids and adaptations, and so on.

The Southampton study deals with a situation in which social work services for a large populous area had been divided between an 'intake-team', doing all duty and short-term work, and two long-term teams. This pattern of organisation is clearly particularly suited to the designation of a welfare rights specialist within the intake team. In other areas where all work is organised territorially with comparatively small 'patch' teams combining duty, short-term and long-term work the case for a full-time welfare rights specialist may be much harder to establish.

Another argument against welfare rights specialisation is that 'cases' are not readily divisible in a way which enables material-need problems to be given separate attention. People come to social services departments facing mixtures of material problems with other kinds of problems. Material problems are often seen as the 'presenting problems'—real enough, most modern social workers agree, but nevertheless overlying other problems. People most readily ask for help with straightforward material problems, but want also to talk about other, deeper ones. A good social work relationship may entail working through and hopefully solving these presenting problems but then moving on to other issues.

The evidence from Southampton suggests that many material problems are dealt with as such, and that is that. Southampton is by no means alone in this respect. It may be that such cases are not receiving further social work help because there are no deeper problems, it may be because social workers are not able to go deeper, or it may be because social services department resources do not allow them to go deeper. There is extensive scope for controversy here about the feasibility and justifiability of screening for further problems, just as there is surrounding much medical screening. The reality is that a high proportion of those asking for help with material problems get just that, or less, and do not receive an extended social work service.

However, it may be that, to use the Southampton data again as an example, one of the crucial social work skills present in the intake team is a capacity to distinguish, from the host of material need referrals, a minority who need more intensive social work help. After all a small minority of these referrals do become long-term cases. Three per cent were still open after six months and 1 per cent after a year, and even these figures are a little misleading since there were also re-referrals when 'signals' not picked up on an initial occasion might have been subsequently noted. The question is, therefore, might a welfare rights specialist have been less able to detect problems outside his own direct remit?

Again this is an emotive and controversial issue. We do not presume to make any judgement on social workers' diagnostic skills, or to comment on the dangers, discussed by Mayer and Timms (1970), of going from material issues to other ones which clients may not see as relevant to their predicaments. What we do want to suggest, however, is that this argument raises important considerations about the organisation of the role of the welfare rights specialist. Obviously one of the safeguards against the problem discussed above is for such specialists to be trained social workers. But it has been suggested that this raises the problem of scarce skills. In many cases the real choice may be between the use of an untrained social worker for generic tasks or the use of a welfare rights worker to relieve the strain upon qualified social workers. Moreover, specialisation may equally 'put the blinkers' upon a qualified worker. It seems to us more important to guard against this problem by ensuring that welfare rights specialists are given some training to help them spot warning signs justifying referrals to others, just as social workers need to be able to spot situations in which the technical and legal aspects of welfare rights problems are taking them out of their depth. It is also important that such specialists are fully integrated within social work teams so that they can readily discuss problems with colleagues. It is particularly important for them to be properly supervised so that they can discuss matters they do not understand, and so that they are forced to explain to a senior what occurs in their more difficult cases. Thus it may be that the correct response to this 'diagnostic' objection to welfare rights specialisation is the same as that to many other worries about the low level of expertise at the 'coal face' within social work teams—that is, good supervision, and efforts to ensure that workers are not isolated with their own cases but are members of a team, in which sharing helps to reduce the problems of differential and dispersed expertise.

Local authorities are beginning to employ welfare rights specialists. At present most of them are seen as either resource persons to whom social workers can go for advice with difficult cases or as development staff whose task it is to further initiate responses, both from within the department and from the community at large, to welfare rights problems. The discussion here has dealt with an alternative, but not incompatible, way of using welfare rights expertise, as a specialism in direct work with clients within field teams.

CONCLUSIONS

In giving attention to the issue of 'social work and money' this book has concentrated upon two particular problems: the powers of social workers, or at least their departments, to make money payments under Section 1 of the Children and Young Persons Act, 1963, Section 12 of the Social Work (Scotland) Act, 1968, and related legislation in Northern Ireland; and the relationship between social workers and their responsibilities and those of the SBC and its staff. These seem to us to be the core issues, and they are the ones in which *money* as such is likely to be involved. But

there are many related issues which have not been given attention.
In the first category are the multiplicity of situations in which social
workers are involved with the powers of their departments to
decide whether clients should have various benefits in kind—
residential places, day care, telephones, aids and adaptations for
the disabled, the services of home helps, and so on. One might also
even add to this list, their own services, which are after all costly
resources which are strictly rationed by their decisions and the
policies of their superiors. In the second category are relationships
with many other agencies with powers to grant resources, or to take
a gentle line on debts, in which material benefits if not actual
money is at stake, and with whom social workers often intervene on
behalf of clients. The special issue of fuel debts is discussed in the
Appendix. The major gap here is the absence of discussion of
relationships with housing departments. At the time of writing the
Housing (Homeless Persons) Act has just been passed, and there is
a great deal of uncertainty about the way in which this will affect
the role of, and relationships between, social services and housing
departments.

Readers of this book should bear in mind these many other areas
of work, and consider whether the issues raised, and the problems
discussed, about contemporary practice on money payments, on
dealings with the SBC and on fuel debts, are applicable there too. It
seems to us that the issues considered raise some fundamental
questions about the ways in which social workers operate in social
services departments, and about the definition of the social work
task.

We are conscious that we have taken two specific, and related,
ingredients of the social work task and have discussed them largely
in isolation from others. We have tried to avoid the weakness,
which has spoilt some other considerations of these issues, of
assuming that they are the most important aspects of the social
work task. Nevertheless, we have made it clear that we consider
that social services departments should not disregard the extent to
which clients look to them for solutions to material problems. We
have suggested that solutions of the conflict between the pressure
of clients with such problems and the other, undiscussed, aspects of
social work lie in patterns of organisation which recognise the
separate issues involved. Had we looked at social work with
reference to the need to perform some other part of the task
adequately, we are conscious that we might have come across ways
in which the organisational arrangements we have been suggesting
might be in conflict with other social work goals. But we consider it

more likely that realistic responses to 'welfare rights' issues will free some social work resources for other tasks.

The book has analysed contemporary practice on some key welfare issues, and has discussed many suggestions for the solutions of problems which arise with that practice. It has not been written as a guide for social workers, or social work students, on how to proceed when faced by clients with material problems. But it is hoped that those who are looking for such guidance will have found much in it to help them to make up their minds about how they should proceed. In the last analysis the problems discussed are so closely linked with crucial ideological dilemmas for social workers and for those who determine social policy that fundamental political choices are involved. For us, the two central points are the strong grounds for unease about the way in which Sections 1 and 12 are implemented, and the need to give welfare advice and advocacy work a position within social services departments in which it is acknowledged as a specialism in its own right and not just something that 'gets in the way of', or 'gets confused with', 'real social work'.

Appendix

The Fuel Debt Problem

INTRODUCTION

It has been shown that some of the most difficult issues with which social workers have to deal, and which raise problems for the relationship between the social services departments and the SBC, arise out of clients' difficulties in meeting fuel debts. While it would not be appropriate to analyse this in the main body of the text, this appendix has been provided to enable readers who are particularly concerned about fuel debts to follow through the complex policy issues involved.

This issue has assumed particularly severe proportions recently for three reasons. There have been increases in fuel prices out of proportion to the rise in the cost of living, as a consequence of the dramatic rise in oil prices and the phasing out of subsidies to the other fuel industries. Much housing was designed and built at a time when fuel prices were relatively low, so little attention was given to their impact upon fuel consumption. Most fuel bills are paid in arrears; therefore families facing heavy pressure on their incomes as all prices rise are particularly prone to draw upon savings for these bills to meet more pressing needs.

To explain the way in which the fuel debt problem arises out of an interaction of policies with deleterious consequences for low-income families we must look at the roles played by various agencies.

FUEL PRICING POLICIES

In 1967 the White Paper *Nationalised Industries: A Review of Economic and Financial Objectives* stressed the need for the public utilities to adopt pricing policies which put internal efficiency as the paramount objective. They were to operate as commercial undertakings. The emphasis in fuel pricing policies since about that time has been to maximise returns. A particular feature has been charging policies which discriminate in favour of the large consumer. In particular tariffs have been biased in favour of industrial users. For example, in 1975-6 industry was charged an average of 5.2p per therm for gas. It used 45 per cent of the gas produced and contributed 23 per cent of the industry's revenue. By contrast domestic consumers paid an average of 14.4p per therm, using 44 per cent of the gas consumed but providing 64 per cent of the revenue.

There has also been a tendency to discriminate in favour of the large domestic consumer. Until 1976 the gas boards operated a special 'gold star' tariff to provide cheaper gas to larger consumers, broadly households with central heating. The electricity boards have similarly favoured households with night storage heating. All domestic consumers of electricity have also had to face a rapidly rising 'fuel cost adjustment'; this is an addition to their bill to take account of the rising prices charged by the Central Electricity Generating Board, which increases the share of the total bill which they pay.

A number of studies have demonstrated that the poor spend a higher proportion of their income on fuel than other families. The National Consumer Council suggested that in 1975-6 families with incomes of not more than 20 per cent above SBC scale rates spent, on average, 12 per cent of their income on fuel. Households with incomes of £40-£60 spent 5 per cent of their income on fuel, and those with over £100 a week coming in spent less than 4 per cent.

These differences appear to be broadly explained in terms of the basic need for heating, lighting and cooking regardless of income, and of the extent to which the size of accommodation is determined by factors, such as family size and past commitments and costs, which are relatively poorly correlated with income. But this is not the whole story. Significant amongst the poorer families in our society are elderly people, the sick and young children, all of whose heating needs tend to be higher. These people also tend to spend relatively more time at home. Furthermore, it is the poor who are least likely to be able to undertake capital expenditure to enable themselves to acquire the most efficient fuel appliances; or to counteract the effects of damp, draughts and poor insulation in their homes.

The fuel boards may argue that these points about inequality are not their concern. It is not their function to counteract the unequal distribution of income and resources. The cost of fuel is just one amongst many things for which the poor must budget, and it would be entirely inappropriate for them to adjust their pricing policy to suit the needs of that particular sector of society. To do so would not merely run counter to the directive given to them by the government, but would also mean that the low pricing of fuel would be subsidising the high prices of other household necessities. The basing of prices upon costs should enable the consumer to make decisions about what fuel to use and how much to use. 'Economic rationality' is the ultimate justification for the present fuel policies. These policies should lead to the best possible allocation of society's resources. This argument implies an element of consumer choice. So far as gas and electricity supply are concerned, opportunities for such choice are extremely limited. If a house is all-electric the consumer has no choice at all about which fuel to use. Choice is really only effective at the time of installation, since at any future time the capital costs of change may be prohibitive, and for many council house or flat residents the opportunity for choice may have never occurred.

The logic of the economic argument for fuel pricing policy suggests that the ill effects of that policy should be offset by the agencies concerned with the social and financial welfare provisions for the disadvantaged. The agencies involved for this purpose are: the housing departments who provide the physical environment in which many families accrue fuel debts, the SBC which is empowered to make financial arrangements to cope with fuel bills for its clients, and social services departments.

THE HOUSING DEPARTMENTS

It may be wondered why it is suggested that the housing departments have some responsibility for the fuel debt problem. Local authorities today are the main landlords of the poor. It is their housing standards which help to determine poor people's fuel costs. Yet they, like all landlords, are likely to be much more concerned with the capital and maintenance costs of their houses than with the expenses that have to be incurred to live comfortably in them. While they acknowledge responsibilities which go beyond the normal commercial considerations which may be expected to govern landlord-tenant relations, they, like the fuel boards, have been under pressure in recent years to manage housing accounts in a businesslike manner. On two crucial issues, therefore, their interests and those of their tenants may be expected to diverge. They are likely to be more concerned about the capital costs than the running costs of systems of heating, and their concern with maintenance is with safeguarding the basic structure at minimum cost rather than with the minutiae of 'home improvement' which will seem of more concern to the occupier.

When erecting new houses or flats, local authorities have to be very cost-conscious. The Department of the Environment requires them to build to certain basic standards, while keeping costs within what is known as 'cost yardsticks'. They are required to provide good heating systems in their houses, but within these constraints. The problem is that heating systems which involve the lowest capital costs are amongst the most expensive to run. Crudely, the contrast here is between electric central heating systems and other forms of central heating. The owner-occupier who installs central heating may be expected to base his decision upon both capital and running costs. The local authority landlord will be primarily concerned about the former.

Local authorities are also often concerned not so much with the cost of installation of single systems for individual houses as with the provision of heating for flats or groups of individual housing units. They may be able to make considerable savings through economies of scale, or special arrangements with a fuel board, which reduce capital costs but increase individual consumption costs.

The problem is increased by the fact that a tenant may have no control over the amount of fuel he is consuming. Hesketh comments, on the basis of a study in Manchester, that although the Parker Morris Committee on council house standards felt it important that tenants should be able to determine their own level of heating, the design of blocks of flats often prohibits this. Should tenants turn off the heating altogether, there is a danger of condensation. It is not just the tenant's own flat which is affected, but those which surround it. Condensation leads to complaints from other tenants, higher maintenance bills and the reduction of the life of the building. It is brought about by low temperatures and damp weather outside, low temperatures and moisture inside. Consequently some local authorities prefer to install heating systems which are controlled by the authority itself. During the winter, the tenant receives a continuous supply of hot water and heating which he is unable to switch off. He may have no control over the temperature setting at all, or he may be able to set the temperature level himself only above a certain point. There is usually a fixed charge and tenants have to pay for any additional appliances they use.

Another problem with central heating systems is that their management may be quite difficult, particularly for elderly people and for families whose only previous experience of heating systems is of open fires. Learning to make effective use of thermostats and time switches, and to appreciate the roles of both pump and heater, may be a slow process in the course of which high costs are incurred. Little effort may be made by local authorities to ensure that tenants are aware of the pitfalls they may encounter in the use of a new system.

In this country we have been slow to appreciate the benefits of house insulation. Until very recently houses have been built with very low standards of insulation. There are considerable heat savings to be made if lofts are insulated, cavity walls filled, water tanks lagged and windows double-glazed. Some of these improvements are expensive, so that it takes several years to realise the outlay in fuel saving. Owner-occupiers may recoup such expenses in term of the increase in the capital value of their house. Tenants can never make such a gain. So this is another example of a situation where tenants' interests will differ from those of their landlords. Local authorities will be reluctant to undertake the expenditure entailed in improving their older houses, and tenants will have little incentive to do so. Furthermore, poorer tenants will be unable to afford to do so.

THE SBC

Supplementary benefits payments are not classified into particular amounts for particular items of family expenditure other than rent. In *Assistance in Cash* it is stated (p. 6) that 'People receiving benefit allocate their income in the way that suits them best, and they are expected to budget for their fuel bills, their rent and other commitments, in the same way as people at work and others not on benefit.'

There is an underlying assumption that the scale rates are adequate to meet normal heating costs. There are no special adjustments made to the scale rates to allow for the extra costs of large families or for heating larger houses. Nor do the ordinary scale rates used in winter differ from those used in summer; fuel is considered to be an item for which we budget in equal weekly amounts all round the year. To vary from these simple principles would involve complex administrative problems.

However, exceptional circumstances additions (ECAs) may be given to help with a variety of situations in which heavy fuel costs may be incurred. The *Supplementary Benefits Handbook* states that 'extra heating may be needed because the recipient suffers from poor health or restricted mobility or because the accommodation is damp or difficult to keep warm' (p. 36). These additions, which are obviously largely given to the elderly or sick, are calculated on the basis of a three-step tariff laid down for SBC staff. But they may exceptionally depart from their guidelines and give larger amounts.

The SBC may also give extra help to families in centrally heated accommodation. Additions depend upon the numbers of rooms heated. In the passage of the *Handbook* dealing with this subject, the SBC gives some insight into the assumption it makes about 'normal' heating costs. It says (p. 37):

> If a fixed charge is paid for central heating the addition payable will normally be the amount by which the fixed charge exceeds £2.80 a week. (Up to this level, it is assumed that a person will normally be able to pay for heating without the need for a discretionary addition.)

Thus the SBC is aware that under some circumstances the allowance may indeed be insufficient, but it is concerned to avoid making double payments for the same purpose. It is comparatively reluctant to make exceptional needs payments for unmet fuel bills. It makes its position quite clear in Supplementary Benefits Administration Paper 4, *Exceptional Needs Payments,* para. 20:

> Those who fail to pay their electricity and gas bills over a long period will have their supply disconnected, and those who fail to pay their rent face the danger of eviction. In both situations the risk of hardship may well arise and there may well, therefore, be a *prima facie* case for an ENP. Equally, however, the Commission must clearly bear in mind that, where they have already provided for the expense out of public funds in the normal weekly benefit and any special addition that may be in payment to make further payment is to provide for the expense twice. And to the extent that the Commission make such double payments, they are treating those who for whatever reason have not made proper provision for their foreseeable expenses more favourably than those who, though not less in need, have succeeded in doing so.

The problem for the Commission, therefore, is one of equity. It is unfair on a family who can and do manage on a particular level of benefit to give extra assistance to those who do not do so. The SBC must also give attention to the need to prevent mismanagement and deliberate abuse by supplementary benefit claimants who may believe that they will always be bailed out. The Commission does acknowledge, however, that such instances are a small proportion of the total numbers.

In recent years the number of ECAs given by the SBC to help meet fuel costs has risen dramatically. At the time of the annual count of the numbers of claimants carried out in 1968, there were 143,000 ECAs for heating in payment. At the comparable count in 1975 there were 915,000. A high proportion of these ECAs are given to pensioners (see *SBC Annual Report,* p.100).

By contrast with ECAs, exceptional needs payments (ENPs) to help with heating bills are comparatively rare. In 1975 about 42,000 such payments were made, at an average cost of £22.66 each. ENPs for fuel were about 9 per cent of the total ENPs made. There has been a steady increase in the numbers of these payments, however, in recent years. There was a particularly big jump between 1974 and 1975. In 1974 only about 24,000 fuel debt payments were made. The 1976 *Supplementary Benefits Commission Annual Report* speculates as to whether this upward trend will have continued into 1976 since early in that year it introduced more generous grounds for the award of ENPs but later on accepted new arrangements for direct payments to the fuel boards. The latter development in policy will be discussed below.

SOCIAL SERVICES DEPARTMENTS

In the six English local authorities whose Section 1 payments during the second half of 1975 were studied, only 17 per cent of all payments were for fuel as opposed to 45 per cent for food. But the payments for fuel debts were very much larger, averaging £31.24 each as against an average of £3.28 for food. Hence the six authorities spent £2,312 on 74 fuel payments as against £633 on 193 payments for food.

At the time the data were collected, during 1976, the pressure for help with payments was increasing. Some of the fuel boards were already beginning to refer customers with severe fuel debts to social services departments, adopting a policy that was to become more widespread later. The social services departments were making considerable efforts to resist this pressure. The giving of help through the provision of calor gas stoves was one such desperate attempt to avoid helping with such problems more directly. Similarly, some of the departments were putting heavy pressure on the SBC to prevent the responsibility for the meeting of fuel bills being passed on to social services. A striking case of this was one authority which employed a welfare rights specialist who had devised a strategy for social workers to ensure that clients first pressed the appropriate fuel board for concessions, secondly sought help from the SBC, taking the case if necessary to an appeal with the welfare rights officer's help, and only after that came on to social services for provision of a calor gas stove.

Social workers in all the United Kingdom authorities investigated for the social work task study had been involved in helping clients with fuel debt problems, and had had dealings with the fuel boards in pursuit of easy payment arrangements and delays in the termination of supplies. While in some areas regular payments were made to help clients with fuel debts, in other places such grants and loans were very rare. This is a good example of the very varied interpretations of the statutory powers to give money. Broadly, the authorities which maintained a tight control over money payments rarely made payments for fuel debts. The amounts of money involved in fuel debts were so large that requests for help of this kind would have had to go way 'up the hierarchy' in these authorities.

The Irish authorities were also reluctant to become involved in fuel debt payments because, in some areas, non-payment of bills had been very widespread indeed. The conflict that had arisen between the fuel boards and groups of consumers involved an element of wilful refusal to pay bills similar in character to the earlier 'rent strikes'. It clearly would have led to severe difficulties for the social services authorities if they had become sporadically involved in helping clients in situations of this kind. They were not averse to helping with budgeting problems in some instances in which clients had difficulty in paying bills, but were very unwilling to give out money. In Northern Ireland the Repayment of Debt Act, 1971, allowed the fuel boards to have money deducted from pensions and benefits. This also reduced the extent to which social workers became involved with fuel debt issues.

In the London Borough, some large payments had been made towards fuel bills. Yet even here, in one area, a social worker said 'it is policy' to regard fuel bills as a matter for the SBC and the fuel boards. In the other areas of this authority there was clearly also a concern to limit payments for this purpose.

In the two Scottish authorities the payment of fuel bills and of rent arrears appeared to be the two main uses of Section 12. In both authorities the pressures from increasing fuel debt problems have been an important element in making social workers take stock of the way in which they were using money. At the time they were being studied, the teams were becoming more reluctant to meet fuel debts, and there were disagreements between social workers on the use of loans. The researchers sat in on one meeting where there was a lively debate on this issue with some social workers opposing loans while others urged that loans might reasonably be seen as 'clients' Barclaycards'.

THE CODE OF PRACTICE

In December 1976 the Gas and Electricity Supply Industries issued a Code of Practice relating to the payment of domestic electricity and gas bills. It has two primary objectives: first, to publicise a range of different payment methods available to the consumer and, secondly, to define those circumstances in which disconnection would and would not take place. The payment methods include budget payment schemes, the purchase of savings stamps, and other arrangements to allow consumers to make financial provision against their next fuel bill. Some or all of these methods were available in different parts of the country prior to the introduction of the Code of Practice.

Secondly the Code of Practice introduced, or guaranteed, a series of safeguards relating to disconnection. These are as follows:

Before disconnecting for debts, the industries will take steps to
  (a) remind the consumer that supply will be continued if he enters into and keeps arrangements for regular payments, including a budget payments plan, or that he can have a prepayment meter where it is safe and practical. In either case the arrangements must be such as to ensure clearance of arrears within a reasonable period having regard to all the circumstances of the case including the financial circumstances of the household where these are known to the industries' staff;
  (b) request the consumer to tell the industries and the local Social Security Office or the Social Services department of the Local Authority at once if he falls into one of the following four categories of possible hardship:
    (i) the person on whom the household depends is on Supplementary Benefit;
    (ii) the family is in receipt of Family Income Supplement;
    (iii) the breadwinner is registered as unemployed;
    (iv) the family contains children under the age of five years

If the consumer who is in danger of disconnection indicates to the fuel board his intention to make an approach either to 'the local Social Security Office or Social Services Department the industries will notify the appropriate agency. Premises will not be disconnected within 14 days after such a notification ... or such longer period as consideration of the case (including an appeal) may require.' Furthermore:

> Premises will not be disconnected between the beginning of October and the end of March where it is shown that all members of a household in receipt of income are pensioners over statutory retirement pensionable age unless it is clear that they have adequate financial resources.

The Code of Practice gave formal recognition to measures already adopted by the SBC and seemed to anticipate similar responses from social services departments. The SBC introduced a new procedure, in February 1976, to assist many of its claimants with fuel debts. This involves use of the Commission's powers under Section 14(3) of the Supplementary Benefits Act, 1976, to pay part of a claimant's benefit to a third party. In situations where it is felt that an ENP to clear the debt is not justified but nevertheless disconnection of fuel supplies would cause hardship, a weekly sum may be deducted from supplementary benefit and paid direct to the fuel board. This is the sum considered appropriate to pay for current consumption plus a small amount, normally 50p, to help clear the arrears. The SBC also undertakes to consider, after direct payments have been made for two years, clearing the remaining debts, so long as these were not incurred before the person started receiving supplementary benefits.

The SBC acknowledges that this procedure may involve difficult liaison problems between itself, the claimants and the fuel boards. Sometimes the estimates on which the deductions are based may be inaccurate, and sometimes the key problem is a level of fuel consumption so high that an appropriate deduction leaves the claimant with insufficient money for other expenses. In its *Annual Report* for 1976 (p.147) the SBC reflected on this problem, suggesting an alternative approach with considerable implications for social workers:

> In some cases high consumption can be attributed to wasteful use of fuel. But in others, it is a function of the form of heating (usually central heating) in the home. In some instances, the local

office may decide that the claimant cannot be helped or obliged to afford this type of heating by means of ENPs or direct payment. The consequence is likely to be disconnection, with the possibility of provision by the Commission, the local authority social services department, or a voluntary organisation of alternative means of heating, cooking and lighting. It may be that, by analogy with our policy on unreasonably high rents, we should formalise this approach by refusing to consider other than limited and short-term help to claimants whose fuel costs are such as to leave them less than a specified amount for their other needs. The effect of such a policy would be to compel people to move to other accommodation which they could afford to heat. This would be a drastic step. On the other hand we could not support an approach which gave special assistance, related to actual expenditure, to those with high levels of consumption. This, apart from its administrative cost, would tend to discriminate against those in full-time work to whom such assistance is not available, might encourage the allocation of families on supplementary benefit to houses which were expensive to heat, and would be an incentive to the wasteful use of fuel. It would also tend to distract attention from the fundamental problems of excessively expensive heating systems, insulation and fuel pricing.

Two reports published during 1976 urged the SBC to go further in giving help to people with problems in paying for fuel. These were a report from the Select Committee on Nationalised Industries and a National Consumer Council report. They suggested ways of extending the support provided for some claimants by means of exceptional circumstances additions, arguing that all benefits should be increased by the amount of the lower- or middle-rate heating addition. The NCC also argued that people who were heavy consumers of fuel should receive additions. They based this argument on the mistaken assumption that there was a standard amount allowed for fuel within the basic supplementary benefits scale rates.

Both reports also suggested that the SBC should help poor families who are not in receipt of regular weekly benefits. The SBC is very reluctant to do this except in most unusual circumstances. This aspect of its policy, which is particularly justifiable where a breadwinner is in full-time work, is of course crucial in relation to the problem of equity discussed above. It naturally raises special problems for social services departments.

A further response to the fuel debts crisis of 1976 added another complication. In August of that year the Secretary of State for Energy announced an electricity discount scheme providing a 25 per cent discount on one quarter's electricity bill early in 1977 for recipients of supplementary benefit and family income supplement. This indiscriminate help for some poor people, while others— those mainly dependent on other fuels, not paying directly to the electricity boards, or not qualifying for one of the benefits—get nothing, has attracted criticism. There has also been a relatively poor 'take-up' rate: around 50 per cent of those eligible. Commenting on proposals to extend similar help early in 1978, an Opposition spokesman suggested that it would be much better if social services departments selected families whom they knew to be in particular need. This scheme, and the comments upon it, all highlight the special difficulties in finding an appropriate form of relief from excessive fuel costs.

The social services departments have made no special responses to this issue comparable with those made by the SBC. The Code of Practice seems to make assumptions about its powers, and its capacity to use Section 1 or Section 12, which are not always shared by social services spokesmen. One director expressed himself very firmly on this point (Harbert):

Unfortunately, the safeguard that such a system purports to establish is largely illusory. If only a small percentage of consumers in these categories who have difficulties with their fuel bills approached their local social services department, this would be enough in some areas to overfill waiting rooms and totally disrupt the work of the department. Social services departments are not debt-paying agencies, nor are they in the income-support business. They can only intervene financially in exceptional cases where this will prevent the reception of children into care and the absence of fuel does not, in itself, represent a reason for reception into care.

As a response to this kind of criticism the fuel industries, early in 1978, agreed to make clear, either by issuing with the Code of Practice a further leaflet prepared by the DHSS or by incorporating similar wording elsewhere in the notices sent to those facing disconnection of supply, that people not on supplementary benefit or unemployed should consult their local social services department but 'should not expect to get *financial* help as this is only given in exceptional circumstances'.

CONCLUSIONS

We have shown that the problems faced by poor people in meeting fuel debts have assumed critical proportions in the last year two. Fuel prices have risen sharply, and many people are able to do little to reduce consumption, except by drastic measures which would place many who are old, sick or responsible for young children, in situations of considerable danger. The housing policies which compound the problem have done their damage. Housing authorities would have to undertake heavy expenditure to rectify the difficulties for which they are responsible. The general tendency is therefor for all parties to look to the SBC and to the social services departments to provide solutions. Fuel debt problems are classified as income-maintenance problems, indeed as 'exceptional' income-maintenance problems for which ENPs and the use of Sections 1 and 12 are seen as appropriate solutions.

Yet there are a variety of policies which the other agencies could adopt, without entirely departing from their tough 'commercial' approaches to their roles. The National Consumer Council's report suggested a number of possibilities:

(1) The elimination of tariffs which discriminate against lower and non-industrial consumers. A little progress has been made on this, there is room for more
(2) The boards should lose their right to disconnect supplies, and should collect debts instead through the courts.
(3) Pre-payment meters should be much more readily available. At the moment poor people often find that the boards are unwilling to supply these because they deem the risk of 'break-ins' to be too high. They impose extra charges on consumers who do obtain them. The NCC urge that meters which take self-cancelling tokens should be introduced.
(4) Easy-payment schemes should be more effectively publicised.

Suggestions like these are controversial, and do not solve all the problems, but they rightly remind us that it is not necessarily appropriate for the suppliers of fuel to regard themselves as having only very limited responsibilities in this area of policy.

It has already been suggested that there are difficulties in securing equitable responses to the problem of fuel debts through the social security system. The SBC is currently looking at ways of simplifying its own policies—to reduce the complications for claimants, to produce a scheme which is readily seen to be fair, and to reduce administrative costs. The fuel debt issue provides a thrust in the opposite direction. The SBC's critics are urging it to develop policies which, implicitly, acknowledge a specific fuel element in the basic allowance, just as varying rent costs are taken into account. They also want them to meet the fuel cost needs of poor people who are otherwise outside the supplementary benefits scheme. They are naturally reluctant to respond to these demands.

The earlier discussion of cash payments by social services departments has similarly shown that any shift in the burden of responsibility for this problem to those agencies would be equally unwelcome. Social workers are placed in a particularly difficult situation when they are seen as the people at the 'end of the line' and really in touch with the needy. The reality is that they are at present only in touch with a very small proportion of the poor, and their heavy responsibilities for other social problems of a non-material kind make them reluctant to extend their role. The assumption of the fuel boards, as set out in the Code of Practice, and of many officials and politicians, about the role social services departments can play as agencies which the poor can approach for help, raise, in a quite fundamental form, problems for the concept of the social work task.

References

M. Adler, 'Financial assistance and the social worker's exercise of discretion', in N. Newman (ed.), *In Cash or in Kind,* papers delivered at a conference held in the Department of Social Administration, University of Edinburgh, November 1974.

Assistance in Cash, memorandum produced by Association of County Councils, Association of Metropolitan Authorities and Supplementary Benefits Commission, 1976.

British Association of Social Workers, *Cash Code for Social Workers,* summarised in *Social Work Today,* Vol. 9, No. 8, 18 October 1977, pp. 16-17.

N. Burton, review of Z. T. Butrym *The Nature of Social Work, Journal of Social Policy,* Vol. 6, No. 4, October 1977, p. 493.

B. Butler, unpublished paper given at a short course on 'Specialism and Genericism', 1972.

Z. T. Butrym, *The Nature of Social Work* (London, Macmillan, 1976).

Department of the Environment Circular 18/74, *Social Assistance* (London, DHSS, 1974).

Department of Health and Social Security, *Children in Care of Local Authorities,* year ending 31 March 1975.

D. V. Donnison, *'Under the Safety Net',* comments on Lister and Emmett's pamphlet in *SBC Notes and News,* No. 6, November 1976.

D. V. Donnison, 'David Donnison replies', *Social Work Today,* Vol. 8, No. 32, 17 May 1977, pp. 7-9.

D. V. Donnison, 'Against Discretion', *New Society,* 15 September 1977, pp. 534-6.

E. M. Goldberg *et al.,* 'Towards accountability in social work: one year's intake to an area office', *British Journal of Social Work,* Vol. 7, No. 3, Autumn 1977, pp. 257-84.

A. S. Hall, *The Point of Entry* (London, Allen & Unwin, 1974).

J. Handler, *The Coercive Social Worker* (Chicago, Rand McNally, 1973).

W. B. Harbert, comment in *Municipal and Public Services Journal.*

J. L. Hesketh, *Fuel Debts* (Manchester, Family Welfare Association of Manchester and Salford, 1975).

J. S. Heywood and B. K. Allen, *Financial Help in Social Work* (Manchester, Manchester University Press, 1971).

B. Jordan, *Poor Parents* (London, Routledge & Kegan Paul, 1974).

B. Jordan, 'Against the unitary approach to social work', *New Society,* 2 June 1977, pp. 448-50.

A. Keith-Lucas, *Decisions about People in Need* (Chapel Hill, University of North Carolina Press, 1957).

R. Lister and T. Emmett, *Under the Safety Net,* Poverty Pamphlet 25 London, Child Poverty Action Group, 1976).

R. Lister, 'The frontier problem that won't go away', *Social Work Today,* Vol. 8, No. 31, 10 May 1977, pp. 8-11.

J. Mayer and N. Timms, *The Client Speaks* (London, Routledge & Kegan Paul, 1970).

National Consumer Council, *Paying for Fuel* (London, HMSO, 1976).

J. Packman, *The Child's Generation* (Oxford, Blackwell, 1975).

'Parker Morris Committee', Central Housing Advisory Committee, *Homes for Today and Tomorrow* (London, HMSO, 1961).

A. Pincus and A. Minahan, 'A model for social work practice', in H. Specht and A. Vickery (eds) *Integrating Social Work Methods* (London, Allen & Unwin, 1977).

Select Committee on Nationalised Industries, Fourth Report, Session 1975-6, *Gas and Electricity Prices,* House of Commons Papers 353 (London, HMSO, 1976).

A. Sinfield, *Which Way for Social Work,* Fabian Tract 393 (London, Fabian Society, 1969).

O. Stevenson, *Claimant or Client?* (London, Allen & Unwin, 1973).

O. Stevenson, 'Social services as controllers', in J. F. S. King (ed.), *Control without Custody,* papers presented to the Cropwood Round Table Conference (Cambridge, Cropwood, 1975).

Supplementary Benefits Commission, *Supplementary Benefits Handbook* (London, HMSO, 1977).

Supplementary Benefits Commission, *Exceptional Needs Payments,* Administration Paper 4 (London, HMSO, 1977).

Supplementary Benefits Commission, *Annual Report 1976* (London, HMSO, 1977).

M. Valencia and M. Jackson, 'Variations in Provision of Financial Aid through Social Work', *Policy and Politics,* Vol. 7, No. 1, January 1979.

Wolfenden Committee, *The Future of Voluntary Organisations* (London, Croom Helm, 1978).

B. Wootton, *Social Science and Social Pathology* (London, Allen & Unwin, 1959).

Index

Accommodation, grants for 49
  loans for 34
  payment under Children and Young
    Persons Act, 1963, Section 1
    31, 32, 34
Adaptation of aids for disabled 17
Adler, Michael, on policy for
  financial assistance 70-1
Advice and advocacy in social work
  81-93
Agencies, inconsistency in
  responsibilities 72
  social worker and 11
    advising clients on 81
    weaknesses of affecting clients 85,
    86
Aid advice and advocacy in social
  services 11, 68-80
Aids and adaptations 94
  for disabled 17
Appliances, payments, grants and
  loans for 31, 32, 34, 49
Applications from clients, social
  worker and 38, 39, 40
Area management authorising payment
  38
Arrears of rent in money payments 30,
  33
Assistance on budgeting of benefits
  100
'Assistance in cash' memorandum 47,
  73, 75
Attendance allowance 85
Authorities, heavy expenditure on
  prevention of homelessness 30
  making very high use of Children
    and Young Persons Act, 1963,
    Section 1 26, 27
  very low use of Section 1, 27
  selected for study of use of Section
    1 26, 28
  see also Local Authorities
Avon authority, high use of Section 1
  in 27

Basic allowances 79
Bath rails, provision of 13

Benefits, fuel debts deducted from
  103
  confusion between supplementary
    and other 51
  from both social worker and
    Supplementary Benefits
    Commission 52
Blankets, exceptional needs payment
  for 55
Blind persons, local authority welfare
  for 17
Boundary problems of financial
  assistance 74, 75
British Association of Social Workers
  (BASW), cash code of 57
  concern for overlap with
    Supplementary Benefits
    Commission 57
  policy statement on financial
    assistance 76
Budgets, by local community
  representatives 69
  for fuel repayments 104
  social work 34, 37
Butrym, Z. T. and Butler, B. on client
  categories 12, 13

Camden, high use of Section 1
  payments 27
Casework, social worker problems of
  42
Cavity walls, insulation of 100
Central Electricity Generating Board
  charges 97
  heating systems, control of 99
    in flats 99
Charitable money 43-4
  hospital funds, 43
Charities and voluntary organisations
  resources for social work 18
Charity Organisation Society 20
Child benefit book held during
  outstanding loan 62
Child care officers 18
Children into care, neglect of 32
  prevention by social worker 19, 23
    32, 70, 80